a passion for

pattern

katrin cargill

photography by **james merrell**

Clarkson Potter/Publishers
New York

In memory of **Rufus**, who gave me eleven
years of unstinting love, humorous cheer and
boundless affection.

Text copyright © 1997 by Katrin Cargill
Photographs copyright © 1997 Ryland Peters & Small

Published by Clarkson N. Potter, Inc., 201 East 50th
Street, New York, New York 10022. Member of the
Crown Publishing Group.

Random House, Inc. New York, Toronto, London,
Sydney, Auckland.

http://www.randomhouse.com/

CLARKSON N. POTTER, POTTER and colophon are
trademarks of Clarkson N. Potter, Inc.

Originally published in Great Britain by Ryland,
Peters & Small in 1997.

Printed in Hong Kong

Cargill, Katrin
          A passion for pattern/by Katrin Cargill:
photography by James Merrell—1st American ed.
                    p. cm.
1. Repetitive patterns (Decorative arts) in interior
decoration.
2. Texture in interior decoration.   I. Title
NK2115.5R4C37 1997
747.9—dc21   97-10728
                              CIP

ISBN 0-517-70670-9

10 9 8 7 6 5 4 3 2 1

First American Edition

contents

PATTERN SURROUNDS OUR LIVES. SOME OF US ARE MORE AWARE OF IT THAN OTHERS. A LOT OF US ARE INTIMIDATED BY IT—DO I DARE USE THAT GORGEOUS

large-scaled damask on my sofa, or shall I play it safe and use a neutral linen, or perhaps be a little brave and use a dotted pattern? Then what do I use for the curtains and the chairs and what do I put on the walls? Some combinations work and others do not, for instance why does a little check so successfully enhance a *toile de Jouy,* 'or a broad stripe work so well with damask? It's all a matter of proportions; some patterns just work together, and others are better isolated.

Scale plays a crucial role in the successful use of pattern. Presented with a huge room, a professional designer will tend to use an overscaled pattern or strong color. However, a small room might be similarly treated with the use of a large pattern such as an over-broad stripe, used in neutral colors, or in two tones of one color; this technique helps to create an illusion of scale, and hence space so is particularly useful in small urban flats that may otherwise look cramped.

A passion for pattern sets out to illustrate lots of beautiful examples of fabric mixes and patterns, to inspire you to use pattern more confidently. We show rooms where a single pattern creates the mood, such as a stylized floral stripe used on walls and windows alike, or where one color is used in many textures: linen mixed with wool, suede with cotton, or quilted cotton with crewelwork. This book is a celebration of truly wonderful classic patterns, shown here in innumerable different settings in both the United States and Europe. There are no hard and fast rules here, as decorating is all about having fun and creating the right atmosphere for your own personal taste. So the aim of each chapter is to offer a rich source of inspiration for decorating ideas by illustrating and explaining a wide range of interiors where patterns have been happily mixed in successful combinations, as well as examples where they stand alone in splendid isolation.

Each chapter fully explores its pattern theme, taking us through textures, stripes, checks, motifs, and finally pictorials, including historical information, practicalities, and how it can be used either by itself or combined with other patterns in a diverse range of styles, from smart international chic to humble rural cottages in America, Sweden, France, Italy, and England. Confidence with pattern can be gained through experience, but as very few people have the time these days to try out endless different combinations, I have tried here to gather together a host of decorating ideas based around the five main categories of pattern found in the home.

A roomful of happily co-existing patterns: *toile de Jouy* is visible alongside an African kente tablecloth and traditional striped upholstery is used to decorate a chair.

Included within the book are ten exciting projects that are easy to do, from a painted checked wall to freshen up the kitchen, to an elegantly bordered curtain. Each one comes with a set of clear and simple step-by-step instructions and illustrations so you can instantly set about bringing pattern into your home.

The possibilities are endless. Good luck!

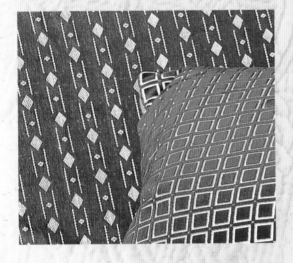  

We perceive texture visually through the play of light on a surface and physically through touch. This is the sensual dimension of decorating, where smooth silk, breezy cotton, and coarse matting all have their place.

texture

TEXTILES WITH SELF-WOVEN DESIGNS ARE UNDOUBTEDLY THE MOST SUBTLE WAY OF INTRODUCING PATTERN INTO YOUR HOME. WITH THESE FABRICS THE PATTERN IS INCORPORATED INTO THE MATERIAL EITHER AS IT IS WOVEN, IN THE CASE OF FABRICS SUCH AS DAMASK OR WAFFLE-WEAVE COTTON, OR ELSE APPLIED AFTERWARD, AS IT IS WITH DEVORÉE VELVETS WHERE THE PATTERN IS BURNED INTO THE FABRIC.

The evolution of weaving techniques over the course of the centuries has resulted in an exciting variety of materials whose pattern and texture is solely dependent on the intricacies of the weave. As methods have become more sophisticated, so have some of the weaves. The spectrum ranges from fabrics such as finely embossed organdy, whose pattern is barely discernible to the naked eye, to the truly opulent textures of richly hued gaufrage velvets.

Left A silk damask pillow cover is bordered with a thick fringe and the combination provides a rich contrast to the chair it is placed upon.
Above **The texture of the cream carpet is its most striking feature; the monochromatic repeat provides a subtle but effective use of pattern.**

Although we tend to be conservative in the way we combine textures in our homes, we find it easy to experiment with our clothing. We need no extra confidence when it comes to wearing a silk shirt with a pair of slacks made from herringbone tweed, completing the outfit with a devorée velvet scarf. So why should we find it so difficult to combine these same textures in our homes? Be inspired by the seemingly haphazard assortment of fabrics hanging in your closet and apply the same principles to decorating. Remember that there is only one rule when it comes to decorating your own home; the environment you create must be one in which you feel comfortable and which reflects your personality. If you want to create an arrangement using a delicate moiré silk in combination with a rough burlap in the same room, it is perfectly fine, as long as it looks and feels absolutely right to you.

Far right **In a small living room, a blend of textured linen and cotton works harmoniously and enhances the lines of the wooden-framed furniture. You can hardly go wrong if you stick to combinations of white, off-white, and cream as a color scheme.**
Right **A detailed view shows the diamond-weave cotton used to upholster the sofa.**
Below **Decorative patterning is used on the pillows, where suede has been appliquéd on white ribbed cotton covers.**

One of the most wonderful things about textured fabrics is the ease with which any one of them can be incorporated into almost any style of interior. As the patterning in these textiles is often more subtle than that of a printed fabric, it is easy to use them in combination with other designs. An interior arrangement combining a variety of textured fabrics in neutral cream and beige displays various levels of relief in soothing neutral colors. However, should you wish to create a more sumptuous room, consider using a jewel-hued damask to upholster your sofa, highlighting it with a matching swathe of draped damask curtain. Whatever style of interior you want to create, there is always a way of using these fabrics to achieve your vision.

The last few years have witnessed a surge of interest in natural fabrics, and quite frequently, visual interest has been created by adding texture to an otherwise plain weave. Until recently these textured materials were considered to be essentially utilitarian, but over the last decade or so they have come to be regarded as sophisticated upholstery fabrics in their own right. Appliqué ribbed cotton fabric, usually woven in white, has a slightly stiff texture and can be used to great effect as a slipcover for an armchair. An additional twist might be to pipe the edges of the cover in a contrasting color and finish the look off with some throw pillows made from the same fabric as the piping.

Quilting is a time-honored method of imparting additional texture and pattern to a fabric, usually made from cotton. Wholecloth quilts, which are actually quilts made from two lengths of cloth sewn together, are marvelous examples of virtuoso quilting skills. The charm of a

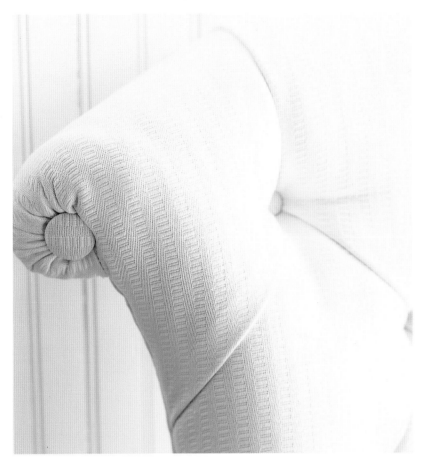

Far left **A guest bedroom has been decorated in a style of the utmost serenity and simplicity. The room has a cooling two-tone scheme and is pristine without being stark. The bed is dressed with a mixture of antique white quilts and linen throws that are offset against smooth white walls and a shiny floor. A pretty towel with brown polka dots is thrown over the back of the chair.**

Above **Traditionally, buttoned sofas and chairs are upholstered in dark shades of leather. Here is a totally different look: a chair with rolled arms has been covered in a ribbed striped cotton in a heavy upholstery weight. The choice of textured fabric is inspired and looks clean and elegant.**

Right **An armchair covered in waffle-weave cotton has a contrasting trim that highlights the elegant shape.**

Left **The exquisite fine stitching of white on white matelasse cloth is shown on the bed skirt.**

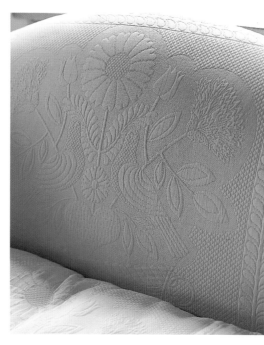

Far right **A light, bright interior furnished with a starburst mirror, antique occasional tables, and an elegant camel-backed sofa (so-called because it is humped in the middle like a camel's back). The sofa is covered in matelasse cotton, which is a thick double cloth with a raised pattern, rather like a quilt. On the floor is a contrasting country hooked rug.**
Right **A detail of the matelasse cotton on the sofa back.**

wholecloth depends entirely on its stitched design. Matelasse, derived from the French word for a mattress, is a double cloth with a quilted appearance that is created by puckering produced by using patterning threads. It looks great used as a thick bedcover or made into curtains, both bringing a comforting note of warmth to any decorative scheme. Matelasse fabrics also work well when used to upholster furniture; the subtle texture provides a sophisticated note of ease to an interior.

Waffle-weave cotton is another material with an interesting texture. Traditionally associated with the bathroom, it is frequently used to make bathrobes, since its comforting qualities make it particularly welcome after a long soak in the tub. In fact, it would be fair to

say that all of the textured cottons work well in bathrooms, where their pile provides an effective counterpoint to smoothly gleaming porcelain surfaces. If you feel that the effect created by layering white fabrics and white porcelain could look a little washed out, try using a contrasting trim along the edges of a shade, echoed with similar braid around the border of your shower curtain. The introduction of a touch of color brings the whole scheme to life.

Although they are excellent materials for making bathroom shades or upholstering bathroom chairs, these woven cottons need not be confined to the bathroom alone. Any white or off-white textured fabric works well in monochrome contemporary bedrooms and

living rooms, where the three-dimensional texture softens the potential harshness of a black and white decorating scheme.

Many lightweight fabrics are now made in such a way that areas of relief are created during the weaving process. Sheer gauze with tiny dots, organdy with flower details, a paisley pattern woven into a length of organza; these filmy fabrics are an excellent way of adding a stylish touch to an otherwise plain room and are equally good at toning down a particular design scheme that might otherwise be overburdened with pattern. The Swedes have traditionally used such textiles with great flair and their vision can be adapted to use with the

Left **Wall-to-wall textures make for a very sensual bedroom. Amid this super-abundance of textured fabrics, not only the walls but also the ceiling are covered with all-over white crewelwork, which was carefully stretched and glued into place. Crewelwork designs typically depict the tree of life, flowers, and foliage, embroidered in chain stitch or herringbone stitch. The use of cloth on the walls and ceiling produces an intimate atmosphere which is much warmer than the more usual white-painted surfaces. Different textures—white linen and quilts—dress the iron-framed bed and the floor is covered with an antique patterned rug.**

Far left **The over-long curtains hang heavily and "puddle" luxuriously on the floor; for the sake of unity, they are made of the same monochrome crewelwork as featured on the walls of the bedroom.**

Below **The rich texture of ribbon lace pillows is set off by the intricate design.**

textured versions of these fabrics. An aura of romance can be created by using flowered gauze to create the hangings for a four-poster bed. This is a style which works especially well when used with contemporary four-poster beds, where the rigid metal horizontral posts can be softened by the addition of long swathes of softly

Above, right, and below **The fashion for animal prints comes and goes, but used with discretion, the introduction of leopard spot catches the eye and need not be a parody of a hunter's trophy. Overused, they can make too strong a statement, but diluted by plain fabrics they add original decoration. Here are examples of a leopard throw (above), a scatter cushion (right) and an animal print carpet (below).**

Right **Large square panels of mirror all across one wall dramatically magnify the proportions of this seating area. The interior is predominantly white, with touches of texture appearing on the sofa and deep armchairs.**
Below **A taste of fake fur is introduced in the otherwise somewhat plain room in the form of a cowhide-covered footstool which provides a small focal point of excess to the arrangement.**

ruffle around the top of a dresser, which will hide the drawers. Sophisticated decorating does not necessarily mean you have to use elaborate materials and trims to achieve a stunning effect; just a few yards of a simple fabric such as gauze or even organdy, if used creatively, can be equally as stylish as the most complex combination

billowing draperies. Another idea for creating a soothing oasis in the midst of an urban environment is to drape a few yards of sheer patterned fabric, or even plain sheer fabric, over a simple pole to create a curtain which filters the light in a most delightful manner. These fabrics can also look ravishing when gathered into a

Left **A mix of textures have been combined in a living room, from subtle stripes, dots, and appliqué work, to an Indian printed cloth.**
Above **A silk and velvet gaufraged pillow sits on the heavily textured weave on the armchair.**
Top right **Pulled colored threads on a formal chair.**
Middle right **Gaufrage velvet is used to cover a stool.**
Bottom right **Curtains appliquéd with a wool edging.**

of patterned textiles, and their calm and soothing qualities help provide a great antidote to the stresses of our daily lives.

Another way of introducing texture to a room is with woven flooring. Inspired by the use of medieval rushes strewn across the floor, sisal, apple matting, and coir have all become popular with

interior designers over recent years. Both durable and relatively inexpensive, these floor coverings work well in all the high-traffic areas of your home. They are not, however, suitable for more formal interiors, except embellished by some form of pattern. Stenciling a border on a sisal rug, for instance, is an easy way to lift a somewhat rustic style of flooring to a level of greater sophistication. There are other woven fibers that can successfully be incorporated into a stylish interior, including rattan and bamboo, both of which are ideal for making sturdy chairs and chic screens.

Although crewelwork is not strictly speaking a self-patterned fabric, because the design is sewn onto the surface rather than woven into it, it does offer exciting textural and decorative possibilities. Typically, crewel work will feature stylized flowers and foliage, traditionally executed in bright colored wool against a white or beige background. Hailing from India, crewelwork was brought to Europe by the

Above **The deep fringe on the chairs adds decorative detail and complements the richness of this stunning fabric.**

Left **The Hotel de la Mirande in Avignon in the south of France boasts this grand drawing room. The very high walls are emphasized with a bold striped silk, and groups of chairs are upholstered in various silk damasks. Traditionally, damask has been used in formal settings where its weight and rich colors create a feeling of restrained opulence. Damask is probably the most sophisticated of all self-patterned fabrics. Ample use of damask can be a bit rich for modern tastes, but a touch of damask in a contemporary setting can create an impression of luxury. Its jeweled colors look particularly impressive hanging in dramatic swathes at tall windows, where the play of light on the pattern creates a subtle textural effect.**

Right **A single tassel attached to the sofa arm neatly draws in the gathered material.**

traders of the Dutch East India Company in the 17th century. These cloths were mainly used as bed hangings or curtains, and examples can still be seen in many of the stately homes of England.

Crewelwork textiles are once again being imported from India to the West in a wide choice of color palette. They can feature brightly hued stitching against a dark blue or black background, whilst others feature sophisticated stitching in neutral colors against a white or off-white background. Over the years the patterns used have remained virtually unchanged, bar the occasional addition of stylized birds. As in the 17th and 18th centuries, crewelwork is still used for bed hangings or curtains, but it can also be used to upholster soft furniture or pillow covers, or even as a novel wall covering. The florid, swirling patterns of crewelwork are thrown into sharp relief when used in conjunction with another kind of textured fabric. A rather stylish example of this would be to line highly colored crewelwork bed hangings with a neutral waffle-weave cotton. Should you not wish to layer texture upon texture, a small checked fabric makes an ideal contrast to a length of crewelwork fabric. A regimented pattern of checks used to upholster your furnishings contrasts well with the soft, heavy folds of crewelwork curtains.

Devorée velvet is a very pretty choice for lampshades. The light filters softly through the burnt-out area of the design, throwing the velvet pile into relief. Devorée velvet is surprisingly versatile and sits just as happily in a stark contemporary environment as it does in a Tudor manor house. The key to using it comfortably lies in choosing the right color for its environment. A pale cream or even a white devorée lampshade would fit in perfectly with a decorative scheme decked out in earthy neutrals. On

Above **A marvelous eclectic mix of textures and patterns in a living room full of warming shades of red. There are soft quilts, a bright floor kilim, and a striped sofa piled with Fortuny pillows.**
Above right **A closer look at a Fortuny fabric pillow shows the richness of its texture.**

Top **A gilt chair is covered in traditional silk damask.**

Above **A similar treatment is used on a buttoned chair seat.**

Left **Rich damask silk hangs on the walls of a Swedish salon. The walls have a two-tier texture, with silky smooth damask above the dado rail and hard white-painted paneling below. The vast scale of the pattern gives the room an increased sense of grandeur.**

the other hand, a devorée fabric in a rich claret shade would look marvelous in an old paneled library. It is not advisable to use devorée for large-scale upholstery as the pile would quickly become worn down and the combined impact of the pattern and texture would be lost. It works best when used to create decorative detailing, perhaps as lampshades, scatter cushions, or purely decorative curtains. It is impractical to line devorée curtains, as this would destroy the subtle contrast created by the pile of the velvet against the flat, burned out areas.

Fake furs, or even real cowhide, are highly tactile self-patterned materials, which are best used sparingly since their impact is disproportionate to the amount used. A couple of leopard-print scatter cushions go a long way toward giving an exotic flourish to any interior. Leopard-print carpets can be fun and have a surprisingly practical aspect to their use; the density of the spots

Above and left **A cushion made from a striped silk scarf sits very comfortably with a bolster on the cool ivory sofa.**
Below left **Large woven black and white checks have been used to upholster an armchair.**
Below far left **The large scale of the black and white check on the armchair are a good foil to the wool carpet below it, which is woven in a large damask pattern.**
Right **A contemporary sitting room filled with diffused daylight is the perfect setting for the domineering oversized pedestal, topped with a bust, that stands in front of an enormous cotton damask printed festoon blind, trimmed with large tassels. The comfortable creamy white upholstery matches the heavily textured carpet; the latter providing additional pattern at floor level. The chunky table in the center is used to display heavy ceramic pots and thick candles, which helps to give this interior a magical blend of the medieval and the modern.**

This page **A modern interpretation of a damask that was designed and printed by Ashley Hicks. It has been used effectively all over the walls and for the curtains of a cozy dressing room. Silk and linen damasks were traditionally woven to commemorate great events, such as victories in battle or marriages. Nowadays, damasks usually feature stylized floral motifs that have been inspired by Renaissance patterns.**

means that dirt and stains tend to be swallowed up. As it is fairly rich in character, it is probably best to combine a fake fur with sumptuous textiles such as velvets, silks, or damasks.

Probably the most sophisticated of all self-patterned fabrics is damask. Its ornamental patterns are formed by the contrast between the lustre of the warp and weft threads, resulting in dull woven figures in raised relief against a shiny background. Usually woven in one color, damasks are generally reversible,

a fact which can be exploited to create stylish effects. Upholster a chair or sofa in a damask fabric and use the same fabric, reversed, to make some pillows. A mixture of different hues of the same damask all used together in the same room makes a sophisticated impact. Damask also lends itself to the creation of dramatic bedrooms. It can be used simply, by throwing a length of it over an old screen to create an opulent headboard, or go to town and use it to make hangings for a four-poster bed.

Right **Standing on a rustic woven apple matting rug is a very elegant chair upholstered in a documentary period print.**

Bottom **The back of the same chair is upholstered in a contemporary check, for contrast.**

Below **The reverse side of the pillow is covered in silk stripes; this illustrates how to successfully combine different patterns on a single piece of furniture.**

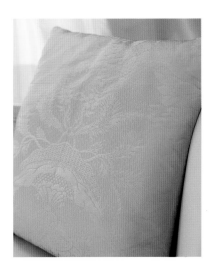

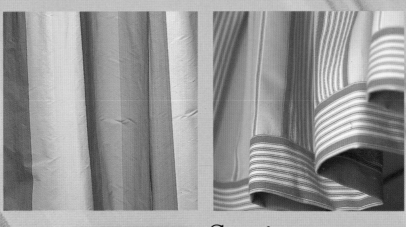

Stripes carry a host of
associations, from sun-
bleached deck chairs.to
men's formal shirts. They
can be low-key and casual,
regimental and smart, or
rectilinear repeats
swathed in flowers.

stripes

Unlike the check, which is almost always man-made, the stripe occurs both naturally and artificially. And, as with checks, it is the impression of precision and order created by the use of stripes that explains their widespread popularity.

Most simply defined, the stripe is a long narrow band which differs from its background surface in either color, texture, or both. It is nearly always the case, of course, that stripes march in groups of two or more, rather than alone. In our daily lives, we tend to take stripes for granted, not thinking about their ubiquity or the choice of decorative possibilities they afford us. In fact, throughout history, stripes in one form or another have been integral to interior decorating. Even at its most primitive, the stripe is a theme which recurs with surprising regularity. Almost every culture in the world uses striped patterns in one form or another; from the simple striped blankets of the Pueblo Indians to the bands of colored clay which are such a feature of African cooking pots. Stripes can also be found in the wooden beams of an English pub, and in the precise alignment of logs which provide the structure for a traditional cabin in the wild woods of North America.

Stripes, generally speaking, are not subject to the vagaries of fashion and always seem to be of the moment. Another of their qualities, frequently exploited by designers, is the fact that they lend themselves so successfully to the creation of optical illusions. On the one hand, long, narrow stripes will make a room appear taller than it really is, and on the other, boldly colored broad stripes will make a room seem smaller. The principles that apply to the use of stripes on walls also apply when making curtains or accessories.

Left The dense, narrow stripes of a straight-backed chair look all the more severe when set against the broad painted stripes on the wall.
Above Painted stripes fan out from the center point of the ceiling, highlighting the modern ceiling chandelier that is hanging down from it.

Stripes are an obvious pattern for textiles, as in their simplest two-tone form they are even easier to weave than checks. Every leading fabric house has its own collection of striped designs, and they make them in all kinds of fabrics, from simple homespun cottons to shiny, luxurious satins. The choice of fabrics and color combinations is seemingly infinite, and a brief investigation will reveal variations on the theme of the basic stripe, ranging from simple stripes of equal widths in dark and light shades of the same color, to designs composed of several different widths of stripes in a plethora of colors. The most complicated designs available tend to incorporate motifs, often flowers, which combine to create the effect of a striped pattern, albeit a highly stylized one, when looked at from afar.

The choice of color is crucial to any decorative scheme being carried out in stripes since it has a radical effect on the final impact. Dark maroon and mustard colored stripes make a very bold statement, whilst pretty

Far left **In this little living room, the walls are painted in wide stripes of similar colors to give an illusion of a much larger space. The two narrower widths of stripes used to upholster the sofa and chairs help to emphasize the broadness of the stripes on the walls.**

Above and right **The guest room in this Swedish manor house has been humorously treated to a regimental military style. Bold red and white stripes which converge in the middle of the ceiling are cheerful and crisp and by extending the stripes up the walls and across the ceiling, one gets the impression of a tented interior. The striped bows and the bedding blend in well to the whole scheme. Bear in mind that an overabundance of stripes can be sore on the eyes; here the plain drapes forming the canopied bed have been carefully chosen to break up the high impact of the color scheme, and lend a certain amount of visual relief.**

painted striped ceiling and room

The attraction of the stripe has transcended many decorating trends to become a perennial favorite. This room, with its wide stripes in neutral colors, looks quite different from the red and white striped room shown on the previous page. Essentially, however, the method you would use to achieve either look is the same. The only difference between the two lies in the width of the stripes and the colors used. The key to a professional-looking result, in either case, is accurate measurements and a dexterous hand in masking the stripes—far more tricky and time consuming than the painting itself.

Materials and equipment

tape measure

chalk plumbline

ruler

marking chalk

low-tack painter's tape

latex paint for walls—either cream and mushroom as shown here, or white for the background and red for the stripes, as on the previous page

8-inch wide paintbrush

2¾-inch wide paintbrush

⅝-inch wide paintbrush

Preparation

1 Make sure all the walls and the ceiling are clean and smooth. Paint the entire area with two coats of cream latex, using the widest brush. Leave the paint to dry.

Marking the stripes

2 The stripes in this room are 8 inches wide. This is a good size for most rooms, but the size of the stripes can be adjusted by an inch or so either way if that works better with the proportions of your room. Measure the width of each wall and divide it into 8-inch sections, making marks at the top of each wall. If the walls are not exactly divisible by your chosen measurement, increase the breadth of the stripes by fractional increments towards the center of the wall. This should be done in such a subtle way that these increases in width are not notice-able. Using a plumbline, mark the lines in chalk. If the walls are perfectly straight, you

can dispense with the plumbline and mark 8-inch wide stripes halfway down the walls and at the bottom; join these marks vertically using a ruler. The stripes that have been painted in the red and white room on the previous page are much narrower, being approximately 2¾ inches wide.

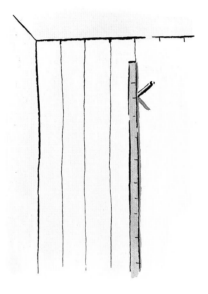

Should you wish to copy this effect, use the same method as described above to mark your stripes, but instead, mark the stripes on the wall at 2¾-inch intervals rather than 8-inch ones. (Of course, you can vary these dimensions to suit your taste and the size of the room being decorated.)

Masking off the stripes

3 Mask off alternate stripes down the wall. Stick the tape to the outside edge of the stripes to be colored, leaving the exact width of the stripes in between.

Painting the stripes

4 Carefully paint in the alternate stripes in your chosen color, using a brush to fit the width of your stripes. Let it dry thoroughly before applying a second coat. When completely dry, slowly and very carefully peel away the tape.

Marking and painting the ceiling

5 Find the center of the ceiling and mark it. This will be used as a vanishing point for the stripes. Use either a long ruler or a chalk plumbline to draw the lines from the stripes on the walls to the central point on the ceiling. Use as much care and accuracy as possible to make sure that the lines from the walls converge evenly towards the ceiling's vanishing point (see right). As they reach the center, you will find that the lines have virtually no space between them; at this point you may find it easier to draw the lines in carefully by hand.

6 At the wider end of the ceiling stripes, you can mask the lines off and paint them as for the walls, removing the tape after the second coat of paint has dried. As you get closer to the center, however, you will not be able to mask off the narrowing lines. At this point, switch to the ⅜-inch paintbrush and paint freestyle. Alternatively, mask off and paint every seventh colored stripe, working your way around the room gradually as the paint dries.

Adding a picture rail

7 The picture rail seen in the red and white striped room on page 39 can be added as a finishing touch. Buy the rail in lengths and paint it with a single coat, before mounting it on the wall; here it is positioned 12 inches down from the top of the wall. Once the rail has been installed, mask off the surrounding wall and apply a final coat of paint. Remove the tape after the paint has dried.

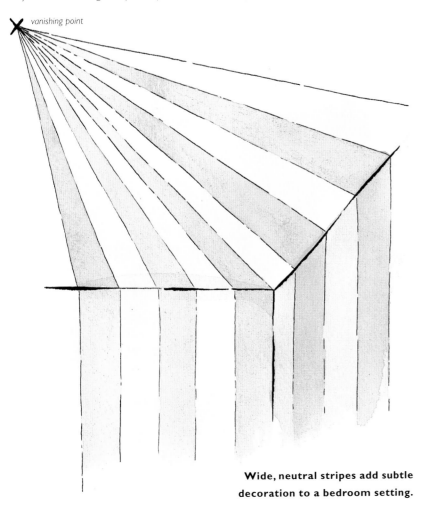

vanishing point

Wide, neutral stripes add subtle decoration to a bedroom setting.

pink and cream stripes provide a much more subtle background. A striped wallpaper in two shades of deep green, on the other hand, would establish an atmosphere of ordered formality. This look could be softened by combining the green with a more delicate creamy off-white. You could use either treatment to achieve a level of

Above and right **Wide stripes in muted beige and ivory give a small French bathroom an elegance that a flat color would not achieve.**
Far right **Much bolder stripes jazz up a tiny kitchen and camouflage a wall cupboard. The shade fabric has been chosen to merge in perfectly with the scheme.**

sophistication in the use of stripes, and it would be wrong to say one was any more successful than the other. It depends entirely on your individual taste and the effect you are trying to create.

Stripes can be used as a simple wall treatment, or if you prefer a coordinated look, you can buy matching fabric and wallpaper, widely available now due to their popularity, allowing you to match your walls to your upholstery, and your curtains and shades. Alternatively, a striking impact can be created by using stripes as a room's main theme in tandem with details such as cushions on a chair or the trim on a curtain that

break up the ubiquity of the stripes by the use of a solid coordinating fabric. This may be better in a small room where the over use of pattern could make the space seem even more compact.

Be bold, experiment with lots of stripes in varying widths and colors in the same room. In contrast to what you might expect, the end result will not be a cacophonous, uncontrolled riot of pattern and the diversity of stripes will create an impression of unity and, if anything, make the room seem larger than its true dimensions. Stripes can also be incredibly useful in unifying a disparate group of pictures. The strong lines can help to draw all of the individual elements together.

One of the most frequently used striped patterns is ticking, which is characterized by a narrow stripe, often in blue, black, or red, flanked by two thinner stripes in the same color, against an off-white background. Ticking is traditionally woven in a cotton twill, a weave characterised by a pronounced diagonal movement. Originally

This page **Stripes are just about the only form of pattern used in the decorative scheme of this house. The wonderful collection of antiques and objects create enough interest without the need for more embellishment. A plain background has therefore been chosen to put the objects and furniture in center stage. This demonstrates how, in some cases, a minimum of pattern can be as effective, sometimes more so, than an abundance of it.**

ticking was used for covering feather pillow cases and mattresses. It was also sometimes employed as a lining fabric inside boxes, suitcases or even, on occasion, in men's suits. A possibly apocryphal derivation of the word ticking gives hints of a sinister origin. It is said that its herringbone weave was designed to keep the feathers inside mattresses and pillows while allowing the bloodsucking ticks to escape. Once restricted to use in bedrooms, in recent years ticking has established itself as an extremely popular upholstery material in its own right and is now available in a whole gamut of different colors, including rusty terra cottas, mustard yellows, pinks, and purples as well as the more standard selection of

This page **Chocolate-brown walls and stark white woodwork, with bright, unadorned windows are a good background for this bed; the Regency-style bed is upholstered in brown and white striped cotton and topped with an antique quilt in complementary colors with plain pillows as accessories. This is a room full of confidence, where the strong lines of the stripes, set against a plain background, result in an elegant simplicity.**

Above right and right **In a large Italian dining room, the old and the new have been fused with great success. The apple green walls combined with cherry pink are easy on the eye. Touches of both colors reappear in accents making this room an inviting place for large family gatherings.**
Above **The thin striped upholstery fabric on a chair is trimmed with self-cording which is also striped.**

blues, greens, and reds, making it a very accessible choice of fabric. Beware of using ticking without washing it first however, as most tickings are not preshrunk and you will need to have them drycleaned otherwise.

The balance and restraint of ticking make it very compatible with the severe lines of metal military-style furniture. The combination works well as the outlines of the furniture are echoed in the ticking stripes. For an attractive variation on a familiar theme, reserve the ticking for the

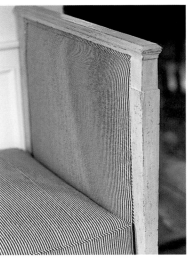

Left and top **The theory that "less is more" has been expertly demonstrated in this home. A period Swedish day bed in an entrance hall is upholstered with absolutely no fuss or frills in a subtle striped linen.**

Above **Simple black and white ticking is used on a curved chair giving it a look of coolness and elegance without detracting from the attractive shape.**

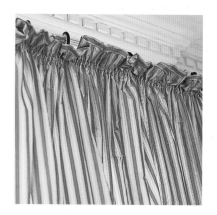

body of the upholstery and make scatter cushions in a standard striped fabric. The resulting contrast provides a high level of visual interest. Metal day beds, typically found in classic French interiors, look wonderfully simple and elegant if covered in thinly striped material. The clean lines of the stripes help them to become the focal point in a carefully considered minimalist interior, proving that minimalism does not have to incorporate a ruthlessly sterile style of modernism. An old-fashioned fabric like ticking can look ravishingly sophisticated in an ultra-modern and pared-down interior. However, if stark simplicity is not your style, don't despair—ticking, or any other kind of narrow stripe, makes an effective foil to an elaborate, cluttered decorative scheme.

The elegant proportions typical of rooms in houses of the late 18th and mid- 19th centuries can be positively accentuated by the judicious use of thinly striped patterns. Let the stripes speak for themselves. Do not distract the eye by mixing them with other types of materials and patterns, such as busy floral chintzes or richly textured velvets. Keep the color palette of the walls, floor, and paintwork to a minimum, and then use two or three different striped fabrics, in roughly the same colors, for the curtains or shades, upholstery, slipcovers, pillows or tablecloths, in whatever combination takes your fancy. The juxtaposition of different shades and styles of stripes creates a surprisingly harmonious effect that also has a look of sophistication about it. You may consider exposing the floorboards,

Left **A small, north-facing living room is livened up with a fuchsia color scheme that gives the whole interior vivaciousness and warmth. The French doors let in maximum daylight and are simply hung with striped taffeta. A variety of different pillows provide accents of pattern, including stripes and sumptuous gaufrage velvet checks.** Right **A close up shot shows the strong vibrant stripes used to good effect to cover a pillow.**

Above **Four panels of narrowly striped fabric are mitered into a configuration of squares to create a stunning pillow.**
Left **In a sunny garden room, a handsome but rather unyielding French period bench is softened with a pair of pillows. The addition of a single central button and contrasting fringe give them a grandiose look.**

either staining or painting them; the layout of the wooden boards will mirror and reflect the striped furnishings by bringing another form of stripe into play. Such an interior is particularly suited to urban living because it provides an ordered atmosphere which acts as a soothing antidote to the frenetic pace of life in our late 20th-century towns and cities.

Stripes seem tailor-made to complement the dignified, restrained lines of neoclassical and Regency styles. Both these styles are characterized by a fondness for geometrical forms, the sparing use of Greek- and Roman-inspired architectural ornamentation, sobriety of color and a preference for linear and flat decorations, rather than richly sculptured ones. Striped upholstery or slipcovers made from cotton or linen were very much in vogue in the early 19th century. One of the most enduring decorative classics derived from that epoch is the Regency stripe, still used by many interior decorators today, which is characterized by wide bands of equal width in two colors and can be

Above left **A novel way to use stripes, is where fabric is upholstered onto the walls creating quite an impact. The same fabric is gathered and hung above a door to camouflage it.**

Above and right **A reproduction four-poster bed is adorned with an informal khaki and red striped fabric. The canopy is made more interesting with an edging made from the same stripe running across the horizontally.**

Striped silk taffeta also looks extremely elegant when made into lampshades. Whether pleated or stretched, the stripes help to emphasize the distinctive profile of the shade. If you want a softer look, a gently gathered shade made in thinly striped material and finished with a little ruffle is the answer. Small fuzzy bobbles are an alternative trimming, helping to soften the severity of the formal lines. Finding the right kind of lampshade to suit wall sconces

found adorning stylish interiors to this day. Despite the natural appeal of linen stripes, stripes made from luxurious fabrics such as silk taffeta and satin can be ultra-chic. Striped silk taffeta, in particular, lends itself to a multitude of uses. It is most frequently used to upholster elegant pieces of furniture such as a chaise longue. A matching bolster with a tightly pleated end, decorated by a silky tassel, adds a finishing touch. A delightful idea for enhancing almost any room is to make up a square pillow from four corresponding panels of striped fabric, sewn together to create a sequence of squares within squares; add a central tassel as the crowning detail.

can be a problem as they need to provide a decorative fillip to a sophisticated interior, whilst also fulfiling a functional role. Striped silk half shades, trimmed with the same stripe cut on the bias, are a stylish solution. Another idea is to use the stripes by angling them across a paneled shade to form a chevron design. This

idea is, of course, applicable to any kind of striped material, not just silk taffeta.

The severity of stripes makes them a time-honored choice as a decorative pattern for formal rooms, or for a study or library where the use of a busy floral pattern would be totally inappropriate. Stripes are the most frequently used theme in classic men's tailoring, so a witty idea is to upholster chairs in the pinstriped material usually associated with suits worn by bankers on Wall Street. This fabric is often woven in a lovely warm wool blend which helps soften the rigidity of the pattern. It makes a cozy upholstery fabric, perfect for any type of soft seating. Add a touch of sophistication with the addition of little black tufts to create a

dimpled effect instead of the more usual buttons found on an ordinary buttonback chair. To complete the look, have throw pillows made in a complementary striped shirting material.

The somewhat severe lines of painted wooden-framed Swedish and French furniture are both particularly well suited to striped fabrics as an upholstery material. The use of a contrasting braid as a border would help to give the upholstered areas more outline and definition. Another way of edging the upholstered furniture

Right **In an elegant Parisian dining room, the designer has chosen the softest multicolored striped silk taffeta for the window treatment. The gentle shades in the curtains perfectly complement the coloring in the mural painting on the wall.**
Far left **The curtains are purpose-fully left unlined so that natural light can filter through them into the room. Because of the lavish nature and rich texture of silk taffeta, the long drops of fabric still look full and ample even without using a lining.**
Left **Lampshades look stunning dressed in silk; here a lampshade makes use of a narrow-striped silk that has been gathered and edged with a pretty, delicate fringe.**

Right **The sofa pillows are made from interwoven ribbons.**
Far right **Striped awning canvas shades are hung between the windows and the shutters. A more subtle stripe is used for the voluptuous draperies, edged with a stripe running on the horizontal (see detail, bottom).**
Below **The tiebacks have been embellished with tiny trimmings.**
Below left **The owner's bathrobe picks up the striped theme.**

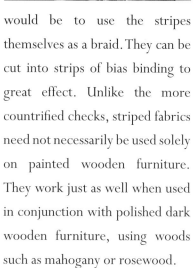

would be to use the stripes themselves as a braid. They can be cut into strips of bias binding to great effect. Unlike the more countrified checks, striped fabrics need not necessarily be used solely on painted wooden furniture. They work just as well when used in conjunction with polished dark wooden furniture, using woods such as mahogany or rosewood.

On the whole, windows tend to have straight sides, and this provides a splendid opportunity for using stripes, which help to accentuate the length of the window. Simple, unlined striped silk taffeta curtains cascading to the floor have a wonderfully light quality that can either help to soften the atmosphere of a formal room or bring a subtly

sophisticated air to a country cottage. If you want to create a more complicated effect, use vertical stripes headed with a horizontal border of the same fabric. A chic decorative device is to make your curtains out of a simple plain-colored fabric and edge the sides and bottom with a contrasting stripe. This approach works well in both traditional and contemporary interiors, and can be a useful foil in a room decorated with several busy patterns. Curtains made from household ticking can be made to look extremely sophisticated with the addition of a simple striped border and caught back with elegant gilded tiebacks.

If you cannot find exactly the material you want, you may wish to consider painting the stripes onto cotton duck canvas. There is something very satisfying about painting your own curtains, and inevitably, they will have a naive charm of their own, which no one else will be able to replicate exactly. A delightfully naive effect,

Top **Three-tone stripes in pale yellow, white, and beige keep the window looking breezy.**
Right **Natural light streams into this delightful living room which just invites you to take a seat. An armchair is upholstered in a coordinating stripe and pepped up with sunny yellow spotted pillows. The unyielding surfaces of the white-painted planked walls and the polished wood floor are easily alleviated by the arrangement of light and airy accessories.**

This page **In a living room, the walls are hung with vellum for a softening effect. Natural tones prevail: the sofas are covered in white and cream linen, and the only pattern is the striped pillows.**

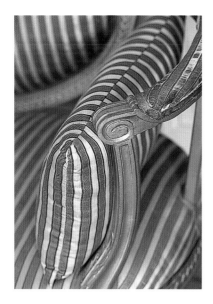

Above **An unusual medallion-backed gilt sofa at Gripsholm Castle in Sweden is upholstered in a rich striped silk, the texture of which befits the gold frame.**
Above right **Two plain pieces of fabric sewn together make a simple broad stripe and an effective use of color to decorate both a pillow and a chair seat.**

reminiscent of the interiors so typical of the artistic Bloomsbury Group, hand-painted curtains look charming in an informal setting in either a country or a town house. Similarly, custom-painted stripes on canvas work well in casual outdoor settings—try painting your own deckchairs or director's chairs for really individual summer seating.

Slatted wooden blinds are yet another classic instance of the stripe as a pattern. Widely used in hot climates, they are an excellent means of allowing strong light to be gently filtered into rooms as well as being an

This page **Elegant gilt chairs in a very grandiose setting are covered in a cloth akin to the sort of stylish suits belonging in the boardroom. Surrounded by the rich patterns of the hanging tapestry, heavy tablecloth, and decorative carpet, this somber fabric tones down the atmosphere, but also manages to catch the eye.**

efficient way of maintaining air circulation. There are even fabrics printed to resemble slatted blinds. These look great hung on their own, but can be used as a "hidden" element, serving a functional role behind draperie that are always left open, where they act as a visual frame for the window.

Decorative trimmings can be added to a shade as a flourish. A scalloped border, or a fringe of tassels, is an ingenious way of softening the rigidity of a striped shade. Use the

same device elsewhere in the room, perhaps along the bottom of a slipcover on a sofa or armchair, or around the edge of a tablecloth. The effect achieved by using a repeated trim is a dramatic but also a simple way of drawing together the overall decorative scheme of a room.

Another way of using stripes is to upholster a chair with wide contrasting bands of a plain material, reversing the stripes on the back. For a formal room try different shades of brown or gray or, if your goal is a knock-out look, try using white striped with bright primary colors, like scarlet, sulfur, or ultramarine. These color combinations are very

Left **A trio of Gustavian chairs. These beautifully shaped chairs are neoclassical in style; their design was most popular during the short reign of the Swedish ruler Gustav II (1771-92) and today this style of furniture is making a comeback well beyond the borders of Sweden. Similarly scaled stripes and checks are the ideal choice of upholstery for this style of furniture as these relatively low-key patterns allow the outline and detail of the carved wood to stand out.**

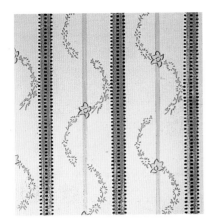

Below **Florid striped wallpaper, a replica of a 19th-century pattern, is used courageously to cover awkward contours in this room. The wallpaper camouflages an angled chimney flue and even hides a sizeable stove pipe.**
Left and below right **A rather less exuberant, but extremely pretty look, is created with a more delicate Swedish wallpaper, designed to look like stenciling.**

effective used to cover pillows and are an excellent way of using up leftover fabric. Children's rooms in particular benefit from this bold approach, the direct simplicity helping to create a warm and cheerful environment.

Screens are another useful decorating device, especially in dressing rooms, bedrooms, or bathrooms, where they can be an ingenious and stylish way of hiding unsightly sinks or crowded racks of clothing. The tailored lines and the rigidly rectangular panels of screens are ideally suited to being covered in material in a variety of stripes, either thin, bold, floral, or even a mixed pattern that uses both florals and stripes together; the possibilities are endless.

Add a sophisticated flourish to your screen by edging it with a decorative and handsome braid, or

painted kitchen wall

This charming painted motif is fairly easy to achieve by following a few simple steps. You might like to try out some of the more complicated techniques first before starting on your walls. Do remember though that the slightly naive feel of this pattern is part of its inherent charm, so try to work freestyle and don't worry too much about any minor imperfections.

Materials and equipment

tape measure

latex paint in cream

paintbrush for base coat

12-inch long card template

pencil

chalk

chalk plumbline

stencil cardboard for
two 24 x 4-inch strips

compass

scalpel or craft knife

spray adhesive

white acrylic or stencil paint

sponge

fine-tip artist's brush

moleskin acrylic or stencil paint

low-tack painter's tape

yellow acrylic scumble glaze

3½-inch wide paintbrush

artist's graining comb or cardboard
with comb cut into it

¼-inch wide paintbrush

dark yellow acrylic scumble glaze

flat-finish varnish

Planning the layout

1 Because the proportions of rooms vary so much, you must take the dimensions of your particular room into account before planning your design. The size of the stripes given in the method detailed below were worked out by dividing the width of the main wall by the number of repeats desired. In this case, the wide stripes are 4 inches across and the narrow stripes are 2½ inches across. Bear in mind, however, that this particular room is a small-to-average sized kitchen and the stripes were proportioned accordingly. If the room you are painting is very large, you may wish to double the proportions given here.

If the measurements do not work out exactly on all four walls of the room you are painting, adjust the width of your stripes by tiny increments or reductions; otherwise, you may end up with a corner where your stripes converge, spoiling the overall effect.

Preparation

2 Paint the whole room with two coats of cream-colored satin latex paint.

Marking the lines

3 Mark a sequence of stripes (one wide stripe, one narrow stripe, another wide stripe, and so on) on your template.

Place the middle of this cardboard strip on the center of the wall, close to the junction of the wall and ceiling. Mark the vertical

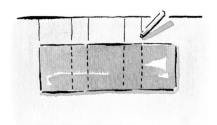

edges of the stripes with chalk. Continue making these marks, going out to the corners of the wall in each direction. Drop the chalk plumbline down from each mark to create the vertical guide lines.

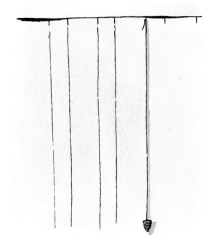

Preparing the stencil

4 Cut out a strip of stencil card the width of the wide stripe and long enough to fit in four dots. In this example there is a 6-inch gap between each dot, so you will need a 24-inch length of card. Mark each strip into four rectangles and draw a cross meeting in the center of each of these rectangles. Place a compass at this centre point and use it to draw a circle with a circumference of 1 inch. Cut the circles out of the rectangles with a scalpel or craft knife.

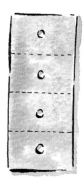

Stenciling onto the wall

5 Spray the back of the stencil with spray adhesive. Place the stencil at the top of the wall over one of the wide stripes. Dab a small amount of white acrylic or stencil paint on your sponge and then dab it gently over the holes. When the paint has dried, reposition the stencil, placing the top circle over the lowest painted one as a positioning guide. Continue working the stencil down the wall. Wash your brush or sponge out after each drop in order to prevent a build-up of paint.

6 For the next wide stripe, position the stencil 3 inches further down the wall so that the dots are staggered. Continue stenciling the dots this way, staggering the heights of the first dot on each alternate band.

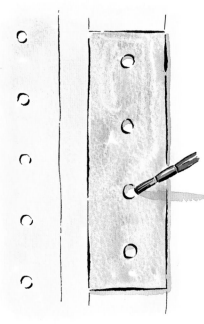

7 To create the shadow effect around each dot, dip your fine brush into the moleskin paint and paint a small crescent moon shape around the bottom left-hand side of each stenciled dot. Let dry completely.

Combing in the wavy lines

8 Mask off the sides of the wide stripes. Use the yellow scumble glaze and the 3½-inch

wide brush to paint a stripe the width of the brush over the stenciled dots.

9 Using the artist's graining comb, wiggle it gently downward in one movement over the top of the scumble glaze to create a wavy line. Repeat this process for each wide band. Let it dry and remove the tape.

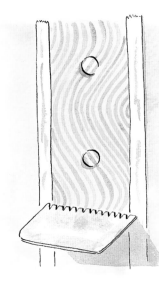

Painting the freestyle lines

10 Using the narrowest brush and the dark yellow scumble glaze, paint freestyle along the chalk lines to mark out the stripes.

Finishing off

11 Apply a coat of flat varnish over the whole painted area.

A row of plates hung down one of the stripes mimics the effect of the dots painted in the other panels.

use old-fashioned brass nails to make an interesting and unusual border, either in a single or double row.

Although stripes are usually found as solid bands of contrasting color, you should never restrict yourself to a plain spectrum when using them. There are any number of patterns which appear to be striped, but on closer examination can be seen to incorporate repeating motifs or do not lie in strict parallel lines. Ever since the 18th century, both in the United States and in Europe, there has been a constant demand for such stylized striped patterns, for use as wallpapers, upholstery fabrics, or as a painted motif. The appeal of these designs is that the overall effect is not as formal as a pattern made up of pure, straight stripes. Some of these stylized stripes are interspersed with little floral motifs, others have wavy lines which alternate with a figurative motif, and yet more have a pattern of wavy floral stripes, vertically arranged like a series of snakes climbing up the fabric. The use of such fabrics as wall coverings tends to work best when they are employed in conjunction with fairly formal furniture. Used in this combination, the stylized fabric design plays an important role, bringing a softening element into an otherwise somewhat severe decorative scheme. Again, just as plain stripes can create an illusion of

This page **A striped effect can be created by repeating wavy lines as well as just using rectilinears. The pictures on this page and the main photograph show a few examples of French fabrics that are either printed or woven in complex but repeating stripes, using a variety of colors and decorative motifs to cover walls and upholster furniture.**

and a popular combination results from the use of a floral stripe as an upholstery fabric on wooden-framed armchairs or *fauteuils,* as well as covering the wall above the dado rail. A scheme such as this would typically be finished off with a set of matching curtains. The combination of walls paneled with wood up to the height of the dado rail and the floral striped fabric used to upholster the wall

height, so can these striped floral fabrics, but they do so in a less obvious manner. In fact, stylized stripes can look really good in any type of room, from a small bathroom to a spacious living room. When using them though, remember that the scale and density of the pattern are of paramount importance to the finished effect created by the decorative scheme.

Extremely popular in France, the stylized stripe complements the elegant formality that is characteristic of many French decorative schemes. The French love to use the same fabric on several surfaces in the same room,

Above **On a sunny Provençal terrace, meals are served on elegant wrought-iron furniture with comfortable cushions covered in a woven stylized stripe.**

above, helps to keep the overall effect from being too pretty, although the effect still manages to have a very delicate flavour to it. The key to the success of such a scheme is the use of the stylized stripe, as by using several patterns within each stripe, it prevents the extensive use of the same design from overwhelming the eye.

The drawback to these striped floral designs is that it can be hard to visualize the final effect from the small fabric swatches given out by fabric houses. It is worth investing in a yard or two first, giving you enough fabric to make a realistic assessment of its overall impact. If you do not want to use fabric to cover your walls, you will find that many patterns are available as wallpapers as well. When choosing your pattern, think of the scale of the room—a loftily proportioned room needs a boldly scaled pattern for it to make any impact and the use of a more subtle stripe may cause a blurring effect on the walls and waste the use of a delicate pattern.

Left and below **For a lively interior, French cotton stripes cover the walls and sofa to create a welcoming, cozy room. The colors work well together: busy floral stripes are toned down with a miniature check and the accessories are set off with bright-blue painted woodwork.**
Middle left **A pair of bérgère chairs placed beside a tall window are covered in chevron striped cotton matching the long curtains. The color scheme blends in well with the floor, which is covered in a striking checked pattern.**
Far left **Woven bargello tapestry linen is used to upholster a chair and stands out against a plain wall.**

Above **An intricate French wallpaper uses stylized flowers.**
Middle right **This room in a small French 18th-century chateau displays carved and gilded paneling and the sofa is embellished simply with blue and white printed cloth in a lattice pattern.**
Bottom right **Inside a Swedish castle, a woven pattern of floral stripes surrounds an alcove bed.**
Far right **Because of their high ceilings and tall doors and windows, grandiose 18th-century interiors lend themselves beautifully to patterns with some complexity and color. In a large space decorated with period details, a good measure of pattern is called for, since solids would be too insipid.**

Ikat is another form of stripe, albeit one with a distinctly ethnic flavor, which is principally found nowadays in Central Asia, Turkey, and Indonesia. The design of these traditional ikats varies from simple two-color stripes to highly complex patterns based on floral motifs. The most expensive and luxurious type was velvet ikat which combined time-consuming dyeing processes with a slow and

painstaking weaving technique. Bolts of ikat and coats made from the cloth were given to courtiers and ambassadors by the local khans and emirs as marks of distinction or as rewards for services rendered.

Ikats and other such ethnic fabrics are so richly patterned that a little of them in an

interior goes a long way. Use them to make curtains or to upholster a chair by all means, but do not overburden the room with a plethora of other stripes or patterns.

In hot climates one does not feel the need for overwhelming amounts of pattern or the deep rich colors of a northern interior. Bold colors, in combination with large areas of white, are the decorative classics of sunny countries the world over. Coolly arranged stripes exploit this affinity and are perfect for upholstery or slipcovers in the strong light of mediterranean or tropical countries. Outdoor furniture, or seating arranged near large windows or doors that receive large amounts of sunlight, look good in fabric which combines

Left and above **An unusual print on reproduction chairs with a complementary print used for the walls and curtains.**
Far left **Stripes in more guises: a black and cream pattern in repeating stripes covers the walls, with the same design used to edge the cream curtains.**

white with stripes, in bold shades of red, purple, green, or brown. Alliances of paler colors such as yellow and white, or pale blue and white, would have a more subdued effect under the bright light of the sun.

If you feel, however, that the effect of all-over stripes is too much for your taste, try opting for upholstery in a solid color, such as chocolate, enlivened by a chic border in a coordinating striped fabric, or use a stylized stripe to add a touch of decoration to an otherwise plain hanging. Simple bordered hangings can also be employed to great effect around a four-poster bed and the

bordered curtains with loose lining

These curtains are made from plain cream woven fabric and are edged with a strip of printed fabric which matches that of the other patterns in the room. This particular fabric features a stripe which delineates the floral motif, but you can choose any patterned fabric you like to create a border for these curtains. You could make pillows up in a fabric that matches the curtain's printed border to echo the pattern elsewhere in the room. The creamy yellow lightweight lining fabric is attached to the main fabric only at the top of the curtains; this allows you to drape the two fabrics differently allowing the warmer tones of the lining to show through. Light filtering through the two sets of curtains produces a very pleasing effect.

Materials and equipment

main curtain fabric (see step 1 for amount)

lining fabric (as for main curtain)

contrasting fabric for 10-inch wide border
for one side and the bottom edge
of each curtain

tape measure

3-inch wide pencil pleat heading tape

curtain pole and rings

scissors

staight pins

Preparing the fabric

1 Measure the height from the top of your window to the floor and add an extra 1½-inch hem allowance plus 2 inches for the top of the curtain. Cut out each piece of main curtain fabric and lining fabric to this length. Allow two and a half times the pole width when calculating the width of the curtain fabric. If you are going to be using more than one width of fabric per curtain, now is the time to pin and machine stitch the main fabric widths together. Repeat for the lining so that both panels of fabric are of equal size; press the seams open.

Preparing the border

2 Cut out two strips of border fabric the same length as the main curtain fabric and another two strips equal to the measurement of the bottom of each curtain.

Sewing the border to the main curtain

3 Turn under and press a ½-inch hem along both edges of the border fabric to tuck under the raw edges. Position it 1½ inches from the raw outer edge of the curtain; pin and baste in place. Repeat along the bottom edge, positioning the border 1½ inches from the raw edge. Miter the corners where they meet and stitch in place. Topstitch the border to the fabric along the line of basting.

Making the curtains

4 Fold the long sides of each curtain in by ½ inch and then once again by a further inch to make a double hem, press flat. Use a hem stitch to hold the folded edge to the flat fabric; work by hand in small, neat diagonal stitches, on the wrong side, as below. Repeat the hand hemming along the bottom edge, folding the corners in neatly. The border strip will now sit exactly along the side and bottom edges of the curtain.

5 Hem the sides and bottom of the lining fabric as for the main curtain fabric (see step 4). Pin and baste the wrong side of the main curtain to the right side of the lining along the top edge; use a ½-inch seam allowance.

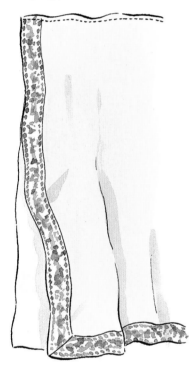

Attaching the heading tape

6 Cut a length of heading tape equal to the width of the curtain, add a further 2 inches to allow for the two 1-inch end turnings. Treating the main curtain fabric and the lining as one, fold the top edge of the curtain to the back by 2 inches and press in place. Now pin the prepared heading tape in position so that it sits ⅛ inch from the top folded edge of the curtain and covers the raw edge of the top turning.

7 Pull the cords on one side of the heading tape for 1 inch and knot them together. Then turn under the end of the tape by 1 inch and pin in place. Repeat for the other side of the heading tape, knotting the cord and turning the ends under.

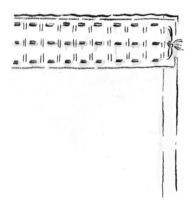

8 Machine stitch the tape in place, stitching along the top edge first, but take care not to sew down the knotted cords at the edges. Stitch the bottom edge of the tape in the same direction as the top to prevent puckering. Gather the tape by pulling evenly on the cords and insert the curtain hooks, spacing them evenly along the length. To hang the curtains, insert the hooks into the rings on the pole.

Add a decorative touch to plain curtains with a patterned border around the sides and bottom, held open with a tasseled tieback.

73

predominance of a plain background would provide a more soothing aspect to early mornings. Alternatively, if you want to use a more complicated pattern, you could embellish it with an overcurtain of gauze, that will gently blur the pattern and create a floaty ethereal look. If you yearn for a four-poster bed but are concerned about the vast quantity of fabric required to drape it effectively, try opting for the relatively inexpensive option of using curtains made out of a reversible woven material that will not necessitate the use of an extra lining fabric. This is a decorating device that would work with any style of interior, whether you favor a traditional or a contemporary approach. It would also look particularly stunning on the simple metal-framed four-poster bed.

Above **In a stylish hotel in Aix-en-Provence, France, the hall is carpeted in a multicolored stripe.** Right **The curtains are made from a reversible woven striped pattern which needs no lining.**

Another fun idea for a four-poster would be to emulate the striped pattern characteristic of traditional barber's poles by painting the posts with diagonal primary-colored stripes. Plain organdy curtains would be the ideal complement. An unusual, but very effective detail can be made by tying a selection of brightly colored ribbons to the finial of each post, like ribbons

This page **In a Pennsylvania farmhouse, a large wing chair has a striped quilt thrown over it, offering a strong and solitary pattern in an otherwise minimalist room.**
Right **A variety of yellow themed silks mix well together in a salon. Different floral stripes sit well in the same room when united by a common color scheme.**

tied around a maypole. It is an easy way of bringing an interesting dash of color into the decorative scheme of a bedroom.

A padded headboard in a crisp striped material coupled with white bed linen is a look that is sophisticated and inviting. Bed linen piped in the same color as the dominant color of the padded headboard would be a neat finishing touch. Let the stripes speak for themselves and keep other furnishings in the room to a minimum.

Vita Sackville-West said, in reference to gardening, that the key to success lay in combining formality and informality; just as a garden's borders are usually the stripes which

Below **Classic French** printed
fabrics mix well in a small seating
area that is part of a bedroom.
Right **White linen bed covers**
highlight the very large repeating
leafy stripe that is upholstered
onto the walls of this classic
French bedroom.

provide formality in that particular context, so, in interior decoration, stripes help to give order and regularity to a room. Within this stable framework, there are an infinite variety of stripes suitable for creating all kinds of moods, from a soothing tempo using a neutral palette to an energizing riot of fairground hues. Using the stripe as a starting point, you can create all kinds of moods and looks by varying your colors and experimenting with the diverse selection of striped fabrics and wall coverings available today.

Left **Beautifully paneled doors and windows in a light and airy high-ceilinged room lend themselves perfectly to a pretty flowery striped wallpaper and matching long curtains.**

Above **Inside a Swedish Gustavian interior linen panels have been suspended to cover the walls and the fabric then painted in a repeating stripe. To create a unique wallcovering you can try this yourself, experimenting first on plain lining paper.**

No pattern is more versatile than the check. The horizontals and verticals can be thick or thin, densely or widely spaced, even or uneven, on any scale, and in any color. Best of all, checks are friendly to a wide range of other patterns.

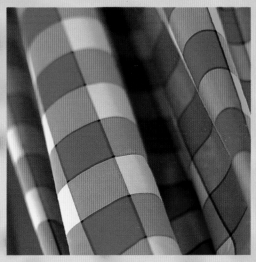

checks

THE APPEAL OF THE CHECK LIES IN ITS SIMPLICITY. THE CRISPLY DEFINED PATTERN OF REPEATING SQUARES IN CONTRASTING COLORS HAS A DELIGHTFULLY CLEAN LOOK THAT IS EASY ON THE EYE.

Checks are a wonderfully versatile decorating pattern: they can be used in every style of interior and in every room, from a bedroom or study to the boardroom. They work just as well when used to make amply draped curtains for formal rooms or, in a more casual setting, as cheery gingham slipcovers jazzing up simple kitchen chairs.

One of the earliest decorative forms known to mankind, the structure of the check is based on a system of intersecting horizontal and vertical lines which echo those of the warp and the weft. Checks of all sizes and colors have played an important role in decorative schemes in almost every country in the world. They can be found literally every-

Above **These bold red and white checked fabrics are enhanced by the addition of a contrasting piped border in a tiny blue and white check.**
Left **Antique homespun checked fabrics, collected over the years, fill an armoire. Use them in combination to create an attractive patchwork quilt.**

where you look, as wall coverings and flooring schemes, in the ceramic tiles surrounding a fireplace and the glazing bars of a window, in winter's wool throws and summer's picnic blankets.

There are no rules governing how checks should be used. They can be the dominant pattern in a room or used as a foil against busier, high-impact fabrics such as *toile de Jouy*. Both styles are equally attractive in their own way. When it comes to choosing checks for your home, have fun and experiment with an eclectic mix of checks in a wide range of different sizes and colors, mingling them with a variety of printed patterns. Swatches are available from most fabric companies and before you buy several yards of expensive fabric, you should use them to try out different combinations in your own home. Don't be afraid of trying out a multitude of different fabrics before deciding on the right one for you.

Mention checked fabric and the chances are that cotton gingham is the one that immediately springs to mind. It is one of those much-loved classics that seems to be beyond the fickle cycles of fashion. We've all eaten at kitchen tables covered with a crisp gingham tablecloth or showered in a bathroom hung with gingham curtains. These days you can even find plasticized gingham toothbrushes to match.

A true gingham has stripes of equal width in both directions of the weave. It is woven only in white and one other color, with the threads set up in such a way that a third, deeper color is formed where the colored warp meets the colored weft. The original vegetable dyes—reds, greens, and a deep indigo blue—are still the favorites for everyday use, although they are now usually produced using chemical dyes.

Gingham comes from the Malayan word *ginggang*, meaning striped, and the fabric was first woven in East India. Brisk trade routes between India, England, and America soon led to gingham being copied, first

in England and later in America. Early examples were made from linen combined with other fibers. In the 19th century, gingham was a general term used for fabrics that included stripes, plaids, and checks; but it was the balanced check that eventually came to be known exclusively as gingham.

It is impossible to think about the way checks of any kind have been used in design without visualizing a Swedish interior. No country is more consistently associated with the widespread use of checks in interior decorating. What is nowadays known as Swedish style should, more correctly, be termed Gustavian style, for it takes its cue from the neo-classical genre which became popular during the brief reign of Gustav II (1771–92). It was a period which marked a high point of intellectual and artistic achievement in Sweden.

The courtiers' wing at Gripsholm Castle is a marvelous example of Gustavian style at its most perfect. Here, in rooms decorated during the 1780s,

This page **A classic Gustavian bench with a matching chair and stool in this Swedish manor house are covered with linen slipcovers in a rich chocolate-brown check. This choice of fabric makes a wonderful contrast to the romantic pattern of the rusty orange wallpaper—an unusual but happy marriage. The informality of the checks offsets the rigid structure of the wooden furniture, defusing the potential formality of the setting.**

hard-wearing, washable cottons or linens in simple designs, often checked, are used with great flair.

The main elements of the Swedish style of decoration are lightness and simplicity, as well as an understated elegance which appeal greatly to contemporary tastes. In a country where daylight is a precious commodity, it comes as no surprise that the 18th-century Swedes developed every possible decorative trick to make sure their gloomy winters did not invade their homes. The overall effect is one of pale colors given a lift by subtle injections of stronger hues. There is a simple, honesty surrounding these classic Swedish interiors which manifests itself as an almost minimalist approach, relying on carefully considered details. Typical of these are the delicately painted features, a little painted wooden stool upholstered in a homespun linen check, or a painted wooden bench covered in simple checked cushions.

The eponymous Swedish check is characteristic of these interiors. With its larger-scale check and additional thin line of color, this is an example of a slightly more sophisticated version of the basic check which sits well in rooms intended for formal purposes.

Yet another example of one of the decorative innovations of the Swedes are chic checked slip-covers. These were an ingeniously practical, as well as being a stylish solution to the problem of how to protect delicate upholstery from damage caused by dust and direct sunlight. Indeed, one of the most widespread uses for checked cloth when it first arrived in the West was as protective dust covers for formal chairs or sofas when they were not in use.

Right **A row of chairs, covered in a green and white check, are lined up under paneled windows that are half-shaded by matching checked shades—a perfect example of how to blend formal structures with informal fabrics.**

Middle left **Crisp checked linen makes a delightful roll-up shade to match the chairs.**

Far left **The Swedes have mastered the art of injecting a note of humor and lightheartedness into the most formal of settings. Here, a chair charms with its casual blue and white slipcover.**

Slipcovers made a big comeback in the West during the late 1920s when John Fowler, of the internationally famous design firm Colefax and Fowler, was designing an interior for one of the company's clients, Lady Ancaster, who insisted that the slipcovers fit rather badly; "Big and baggy," she stipulated, "as if made by housemaids." Today Lady Ancaster's house-maids have all but disappeared, but contemporary slipcovers have

Above **A lengthy expanse of bench has been simply clad in a pale red checked linen. The fabric is crisply contrasted against the mellow tones of the paneled walls. The long, unbroken line of the seat cushion is enhanced by the rigid structure of the pattern.**

Right **Cotton curtains are hung, unlined, at these French doors. Privacy is maintained by the use of blackout shades, mounted on top of each door. Linked by a common color, the checks mix happily with the striped walls and toile fabric used to cover the bed.**

patchwork bedspread

This bedspread is made from scraps of antique and newly woven fabric collected over a period of years. It is a great way of using up remnants, but make sure there is a common theme to the patches of material used, either in the colors or patterns or both; otherwise, the end result could look messy. To pipe the edges you can use ready-prepared bias binding, or, as with the original quilt, you can make your own. The instructions below are for a bedspread approximately 6½ feet long and 6 feet wide, which will be suitable for a double or queen-size bed. The finished quilt has eight patches across each row and eight patches along each long side.

Materials and equipment

approximately 64 patches of woven checked fabric of roughly equal weight, each one 11 inches wide and 14 inches long

scissors

tape measure

pins

needle

thread

sewing machine

10 yards of 1½-inch wide bias binding in either a contrasting or a coordinating color, or approximately 3 yards of red and white checked fabric—enough to make 10 yards of bias binding

10 yards of thick piping cord

8 yards of coordinating backing fabric

Planning the patchwork

1 Lay the patches in rows to create an attractive patchwork pattern, cutting narrow strips off the width of some of the patches to create a random effect, as below, but leave enough material for the ½-inch seam allowance (see step 3). Each row should be 6 feet long, once the patches are joined.

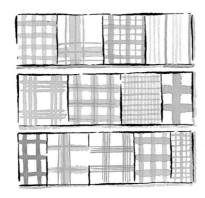

Preparation

2 Baste the patches on each row together to keep them in the right order.

Putting the patchwork together

3 Take the first row of patches and, right sides together, pin, baste and stitch each piece, patch to patch, taking a ½-inch seam allowance on each side. Repeat this procedure for the remaining seven rows. Once you have finished, press all the seams open and flat.

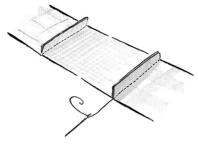

4 Pin, baste and stitch all eight strips of joined patches together along the long edges, taking a ½-inch seam allowance. Make sure the seams are straight. Press all of the seams open.

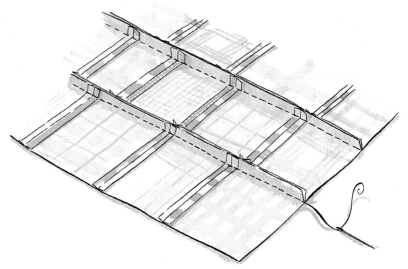

Making the piping

5 If you are making your own bias binding for the piping, as opposed to using ready-prepared bias binding, proceed as follows. Cut out several 1½-inch wide strips of material on the bias and sew them together to produce a strip of bias-cut fabric, 10 yards long. With the wrong side up, place the piping cord along the center of this strip of material, or your ready-prepared bias binding, fold it in half and stitch close to the cord.

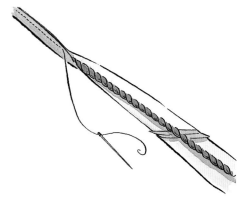

6 Lay the patchwork fabric out, face up, and lay the piping around its edges, with the raw edges of the piping lying along the outside edges of the patchwork. Pin and baste in place taking a ½-inch seam allowance. Stitch the piping along the line of basting and then clip the corners. Hand sew the piping together where the ends meet. Turn the raw edges to the back so that the piping cord sits neatly around the four outside edges and press in position.

Backing the patchwork

7 Lay the patchwork right side down and cut out the backing fabric, ½ inch larger all around than this piece (joining widths together if necessary). Now lay the backing right side up over the patchwork, turning in a ½-inch seam allowance all around. Pin and baste in place along the line of the piping seam. Hand sew to secure and press.

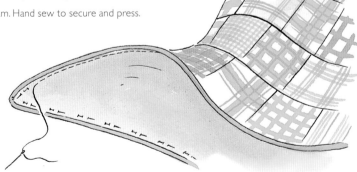

The grid-like patterning of checks makes them ideal for patchwork. Even dishtowels can be used for making a bedspread.

Right **Hand-painted linen panels, busy with flowers, cover the walls of this Swedish room; the intense pattern could overwhelm without the calming influence of the large-scale checked curtains and slipcovers on the chairs.**

Above **An outside shot of the window shows how the decorative qualities of the checked curtains are noticeable, even from outside the house.**

become a furnishing classic in their own right. There is no standard pattern for slipcovers: they can be as fussy or as plain as you want, with ties, bows, buttons, ruffles and long or short skirts that are pleated or plain. Checked slipcovers used on chairs in a formal setting are a clever method of adding a touch of levity to a room. A delightful way of softening up an old-fashioned dining room is to cover the chairs in brightly colored checked slipcovers. The atmosphere of the room instantly

becomes warmer and friendlier, losing any of the stiffness or formality that it may once have had.

The honest appeal of gingham also found favor in colonial America. Its naive quality is very much in keeping with the early settlers' way of life and was well within the capabilities of the home weaver. The irregularities and faults, an inevitable byproduct of hand-woven fabrics, only add to the charm of surviving examples. The tablecloth, an essential feature of every American home, frequently took on a checked form and was often embellished with animal, floral, or hunting motifs. No doubt, underneath the hooped canvas of many a covered wagon heading out to the Wild West, there lurked something made from gingham, even if it was only a simple apron.

Much loved by the Shakers, checks were a physical embodiment of their philosophical ideal. The regularity of this pattern reflected their inherent belief that precision was absolutely necessary in all things to create perfection, which was their ultimate goal. The sect's law limited the number of colors that could be used, but there was no restriction on the size, form, or variety of check used. Unnecessary adornment was considered to be frivolous and fussy, and in most cases perfection

This page **Black and white adds a modern twist to conventional gingham. This black and white bedroom shows how the use of a monochrome gingham fabric can help to unify a complex decorative scheme. The small-scale checks on the draperies are neatly gathered so that they hang in simple folds and make an attractive contrast to the close-nailed headboard.**

was achieved through a structural rather than a decorative design, the key features of which were simple lines, symmetry, and repeating patterns.

The cloth woven on Shaker hand looms was typical of that woven elsewhere at the time in North America. Although the combination of red and black was also found, blue and white was the most frequent color combination, partly because indigo was a dependable, durable dye. Hand

spinning continued to be practised well into the 19th century and hand weaving into the 20th. Many households, especially those of German lineage, had a loom in the house, and the weavers usually dyed their own woolen and cotton yarns. They generally used natural dyes produced from vegetable or animal origins, such as marigold petals, indigo, madder, cochineal, walnut, butternut, and mustard.

This page **The stark simplicity of black and white checks does not have to overpower. The small-scale check used on the walls, ceiling, and window of this room creates a perfect foil for the bamboo-framed oriental bed, large modern painting, and boldly checked chair that stands out with its use of red.**

Long gone are the days when gingham was woven in only one fabric and a restricted range of pigments. These days it is readily available in a variety of yarns and a range of different colors, some sophisticated, others plain. Silk taffeta ginghams, in particular, have a wonderful shimmering quality which distinguishes them from the homespun look of cotton versions, and they lend themselves beautifully to the creation of a more sophisticated look. It is an ideal fabric for creating pretty pillows, gathering into a ruffle around the top of a dresser or making into lampshades. It works well when made up into formal curtains and is particularly effective when used to line the hangings on a four-poster bed. You do not necessarily want to wake up to a riot of pattern and color every day, and checks provide a perfect foil for richly patterned hangings and bedspreads.

A useful tip to bear in mind when using these fabrics is that the most rustic of checked materials can be made to look incredibly sophisticated when embellished with some kind of decorative trim. Astonishing effects can be created by the judicious addition of just a touch of silk fringe or a pleated satin ribbon. There is a vast selection of bobbles, braids and ribbons available in all kinds of fabrics and in every possible color. With very little effort they can be used to dress up anything from bed hangings to footstools. Try experimenting with a whole host of different colors and textures. These telling little details make all the difference, giving a room a uniquely individual personality.

The French, traditionally, have also made good use of checked fabrics in their interiors. A witty idea, inspired by the way they used these textiles in many of their formal rooms, would be to upholster a wooden-framed *fauteuil* or sofa in a checked fabric and to sew on vertical

Above right **Small touches of checks, as seen on the upholstered headboard, add interest to an otherwise neutral bedroom that has been decorated in subtle colors of duck-egg blue and ivory.**
Right **The wooden-framed chair has a large-scale check on its seat which is contrasted by the use of a small-scale check on its back, giving maximum emphasis to the chair's curving lines and demonstrating a successful mix of colors.**

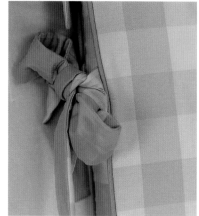

Left **In a breakfast room the subtle blue and ivory tones of this check make it appear to recede. The use of matching blue paint on the woodwork helps to make the space appear larger.**

Above **An antique Swedish fauteuil is upholstered in both large and small versions of the same check, drawing the symmetry of its structure into sharp relief.**

Top **Pretty tiebacks have been made to match the curtains.**

Above **Bright lime-green gingham taffeta is used to drape a four-poster bed. The color of the drapes helps to create a link between the crewelwork bedspread and the simple motif stenciled around the walls of the room.**
Right **The valance is outlined with a green binding and a row of motifs to match the color of the checks.**

bands of floral fabric to create a striped effect. Stick to either French- or Swedish-style furniture which has pared-down, unfussy lines. Do not attempt this effect on squashy English-style sofas and chairs as the rigid surface patterning created by the stripes of contrasting fabrics does not suit their rounded forms.

Checked bed hangings were one of the first examples of an international decorating trend. They were all the rage in 18th-century England, France, and America. But it is to the Swedes, once again, that we must turn for truly inspirational bed treatments as the examples from this era are truly sublime. The look is easy to copy and fits in well with most contemporary interiors. To create your own version, place a bed with its long side against the wall and suspend checked hangings above the bed's long side. You can complete the scheme with a matching checked bedcover. If

Left **The airy simplicity of these lemon-yellow checked silk curtains is just right for this light-filled contemporary living room. The pillows are made in the same checked fabric and add decoration to the plain upholstery that has been used on the chairs.**
Below **The only other pattern in this room is the subtle circle of tiny stars, stenciled onto the seat of an elegant antique chair.**

you want to create a slightly softer, floaty look, use a generous length of organdy for the hangings. Do not, however, be tempted to overdo the ruffles and flounces, since the key to this look is its simplicity.

In 19th-century Scandinavia, beds were frequently built into alcoves, and the hangings served to protect the incumbent from drafts and the cold night air. Today the majority of households have the benefit of central heating, but an alcove bed has boundless appeal for children of all ages. What could be more fun than a snug and cozy corner to curl up in and bury oneself away from the long dark nights of winter? Cheery, cheap, and easily washable, cotton checks are the perfect choice for both

painting a checked wall

Surprising and fun, painted checks on a wall may take a little time and patience to do, but the results are striking and well worth the effort. Suit the size of the squares to the proportions of the room. Generally speaking, the larger the scale of checks on a wall, the more spacious the room will feel. Of course, it is also faster to paint fewer large checks than to work many small-scale ones. This project also includes a miniature check border painted at dado rail level, which breaks up the monotony of the larger checks. If you prefer, you could paint a similar band at picture rail height.

Materials and equipment

cream flat latex

blue-gray flat latex

sheepskin roller

6-inch roller

paint tray

scalpel or craft knife

plumbline

carpenter's level

tape measure

stencil board

soft pencil

low-tack painter's tape

metal ruler

2-inch roller

pencil in coordinating color (see step 9)

Preparation

1 The measurements given in this project are based on 8-inch square checks that cover a 108 x 140-inch area. Make sure the surface of the wall is smooth and clean before painting. Repair any blemishes, such as cracks or holes, using a multipurpose wood putty smoothing it with sandpaper once it has dried. Then apply two coats of cream paint using the large sheepskin roller. Let the wall dry thoroughly.

Marking the pattern

2 Measure the height and width of the wall, and work out a square size that will fit comfortably into these dimensions. Mark a 5-inch wide horizontal band 32 inches above floor level for an 8 to 9-foot ceiling height, to create a dado effect. Use the masking tape to mask off the edge of the ceiling and the base board. This will help keep the painted squares in a straight line at the top and bottom of the wall.

3 From the top of the wall, draw vertical lines at intervals of 8 inches with the ruler and pencil, making sure you leave a gap where the dado band will be painted in later. Then to complete the outline of the squares, mark horizontal lines at intervals of 8 inches, starting at the top of the wall, again making sure you leave a gap for the dado band.

If your wall is perfectly straight, you can guarantee the accuracy of your squares by using a plumbline and level to mark them out. Many walls, however, are not exactly straight or square, causing the surface to be less than perfectly smooth, in which case you will need to make slight adjustments to the pattern in order to compensate for the distorted shape. The only way to deal with this is to mark the wall freehand where necessary. The older the wall, then the less smooth the surface is likely to be.

4 Starting at the top of the wall, mask off alternate squares on every other row until you reach floor level.

Painting in the squares

5 Using the 6-inch roller, gently roll on the blue-gray paint inside the limit of the masked-off squares. Leave to dry thoroughly before peeling away the masking tape, otherwise, the tape may pull the wet paint off.

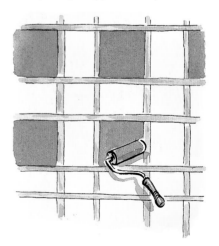

6 Repeat steps 4 and 5, masking off individual squares with tape and then painting alternate squares along the remaining rows—this will form the pattern of checks over the entire wall surface. Make sure you do not paint over the 4-inch wide gap for the dado band.

Painting in the dado band

7 Divide the 4-inch band in half horizontally with a pencil line and mark off every 2 inches along the top and bottom of the dado band. Using the craft knife, cut out a 2-inch square from the middle of the stencil board.

8 Carefully align the stencil against the 2-inch marks made along the top edge of the dado band and using the small 2-inch roller, paint inside the square stencil with a blue-gray paint—continue to paint in every other square along the top. Leave to dry thoroughly, then repeat the process on alternate squares in the row below.

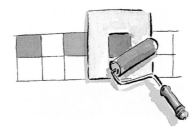

9 Use a crayon (this should be of a color which is darker than the shade of blue-gray paint, but which also harmonizes with the contrasting color) and the rule, to delineate the top and bottom lines of the dado band.

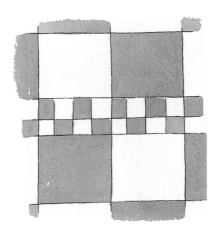

A checked kitchen wall with coordinating shade.

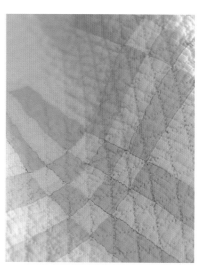

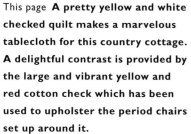

This page **A pretty yellow and white checked quilt makes a marvelous tablecloth for this country cottage. A delightful contrast is provided by the large and vibrant yellow and red cotton check which has been used to upholster the period chairs set up around it.**

bed linens and coordinating hangings. Checked fabrics can be subtly enhanced by using them in conjunction with a plain piped border. Whether you are up-holstering a sofa or just making a couple of scatter cushions to brighten up a chair, you should consider using some piping, just to finish borders off. They look great in a contrasting color: red stands out beautifully against black and white gingham and yellow piping works particularly well used with a purple and white checked fabric. You can also use piping to jazz up a checked lamp-shade or, for a much more flamboyant look,

Right and bottom **Pillows woven from antique silk ribbons, taken from cigar boxes, are an original way of bringing patchwork into a formal living room. The yellow of the pillows blends perfectly with that of the upholstery and the checked curtains.**

Below **The alcove bed uses a bold red and white check as a foil to the assembly of patterned pillows, and as a link to the painted occasional table in front of it.**

consider sewing some fringing in a coordinating or contrasting color around the bottom of the shade.

You can create unique checked fabrics by sewing squares of cloth together to create a patchwork effect. This technique can work particularly well when patterned fabric squares alternate with plain colored squares, or when the patchwork effect is created by juxtaposing a variety of patterned squares. Patchwork textiles made this way create interesting and unusual decorative effects, and work especially well when used as a highlight in an otherwise plain room, for instance as a throw on a sofa, as scatter cushions on a chair, a tablecloth in a country cottage or, more traditionally, used as a bedspread (see the project on pages 90–91).

With their long, dark winters, the Swedes mastered the art of double glazing long ago, so they never had any need for heavily lined curtains to keep out the cold. The result is that one of the chief delights of Swedish window treatments is their simplicity.

Shades have long been popular in Sweden, even in rather grand settings. Many of these were made from checked linen, an appropriate choice of material as the shade rolls upward and inward, revealing both sides of the fabric. The addition of a gauzy swag softens the effect.

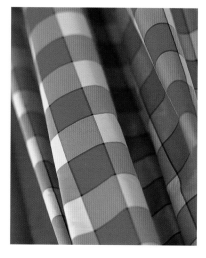

Both pages **These ornately gilded recessed windows at Gripsholm Castle in Sweden are hung with the simplest of checked silk taffetas. The plain check makes a wonderful contrast to the sumptuous damask walls and elegant gilding, but at the same time the rich texture of the fabric is a perfect partner for the ornate surroundings. The windows are enhanced by a simple unlined linen shade in a coordinating check that allows plenty of sunlight in, even when they are pulled down.**

This page **Various strong blues, used in combination with a brilliant pure white, are a feature of this delightful beach house. The assortment of checked, striped, and motif patterned pillows adds variety, but also helps to unify the whole arrangement by using the same simple colors.**

Using any kind of checked fabric when making curtains calls for understated arrangements so that the pattern can be appreciated in its own right. They are at their best hung on simple iron or wooden poles. The plainest curtains or shades can be transformed by lining them with a contrasting gingham check and, if plain gingham curtains seem a trifle dull, a visual twist can be added by using a solid fabric trim teamed with gingham tiebacks in a coordinating color.

Boldly checked silk taffeta curtains can look extremely elegant when they are the only pattern in an uncluttered room. Despite the large-scale repeat of the pattern, the delicate quality of silk taffeta creates a light and airy window treatment that immediately attracts the eye. A couple of pillows covered in the same fabric would help to unify and balance out the room. This scheme works well with a subtle palette of cool, neutral tones. Using ginghams and large-scale checks in strong colors, however, can also be a good way of focusing the eye on a particular piece of furniture. Giant checks used to cover a padded headboard, for instance, combined with a matching bedspread and valance will instantly make your bed the center piece of the room.

This page **The black and white check of the ornately shaped headboard works well with the appliquéd motifs on the white pillows. The monochrome scheme is brought to life through isolated flashes of sunshine yellow.**

stenciled floor border

A simple yet effective little pattern for a plain floor, this is an easy project which will brighten up any room. The original version, as seen in the photograph, is painted white on a bleached wooden floor. The same design would look very striking painted in a stronger color, or stenciled onto an already painted floor. The pattern can be scaled up or down as desired, depending on the dimensions of your room. Always remember to alternate between stencil cards as you paint, to allow adequate time for drying.

Materials and equipment

tape measure

ruler

graph paper

stencil board for 2 corner stencils and 2 long stencils for the sides of the walls

scalpel or craft knife

masking tape

water-based paint in your chosen color

stencil brush

rag

clear acrylic varnish in flat, or gloss finish to match your floor

Planning the layout

1 As always, when using any kind of stencil it is vital to work out the dimensions of the design in relation to the room layout before you start painting. This means that your pattern will be balanced and you do not have an awkward gap to fill by the time you get to the last corner.

The long stencil card shown here measures 20½ x 12 inches and the corner square stencil card measures 12 x 12 inches. Each cut-out square has sides of 1½ inches. The edge of the top square starts 3½ inches in from the point where the floor meets the wall. The dimensions given here are based on an average-sized room, but you may want to adjust them to suit your space.

Start with the dominant or most visible side of the room and work out a grid of repeats to fit the floor. You may be left with an incomplete pattern along the other walls unless you make adjustments by leaving

slightly wider gaps between the squares, at regular intervals, to make the design an exact fit. If you do have to make any adjustments, make them in inconspicuous places, for instance, choose a location along the wall you know will be covered by a curtain or a piece of furniture.

Preparation

2 Before you begin any painting you need to wash the floor very thoroughly and leave it to dry completely.

Cutting the stencils

3 Using the illustrations below as a general guide, make templates for the long stencils and the corner stencil on a sheet of grid paper. Shade in the squares in a dark-colored pen to make them stand out.

squares in total, one in the center and one at each corner. The long stencil can be as long as you want it to be, limited only by the length of the stencil board you have available. However, it is easier to work with one made to the proportions shown here. Always start and end the long stencil with two outer squares as these will be used as a guide when you are moving the stencil along the length of the floor.

4 Transfer the designs from the grid paper to the stencil board and cut out the squares. Always leave a border of the same depth (3½ inches here) along the top and bottom of the stencil (or on all four sides of the corner stencil)—that way it does not matter which way up you use it.

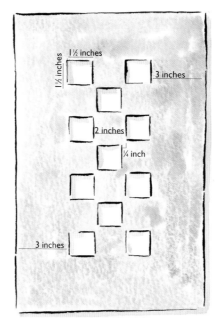

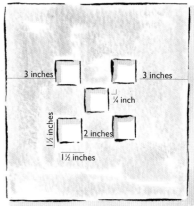

Top and bottom edges of each stencil, to outside edge of outer square—3½ inches
Sides of each square—1½ x 1½ inches
Horizontal and vertical gap between central square and outer squares—¼ inch

Stenciling

5 Start by stenciling in the corners of the room. Place the corner stencil on the floor so that it fits exactly into a corner of the room and anchor in place with masking tape. Dip the stencil brush in the paint, wipe off the excess with a rag, and gently dab the brush over the stencil, being careful not to apply the paint too thickly. Lift the stencil off gently, taking care not to smudge the paint. Repeat for all the other corners of the room.

6 Once the corner stencils have dried, you can start stenciling along the sides of the room. Starting with the most visible edge of the floor, lay the first two squares of the long stencil over the outer painted squares of the corner stencil. Line the top of the long stencil up with the edge of the wall and tape in place with masking tape. Dab the paint over the squares on the stencil as described in step 5. Once the paint has dried, carefully lift off the stencil and reposition it by placing the first two squares over the last two painted squares, lining up the top edge of the stencil with the edge of the wall. Repeat until you have stenciled up to the next corner. Repeat along the other sides of the wall.

7 Once the paint has dried, seal the pattern with clear acrylic varnish.

The checkered border on the floor adds pattern and obviates the need for any other coverings.

Right and top **A perfect example of how checks can be used to subdue busy patterns. The draped canopy of this French bed mixes a blue and white checked lining with a busy floral design and a plain, textured white fabric.**

Above **A combination of checks and florals has been used to create a stunning striped effect on this traditional sofa.**

Left and bottom **A delightfully colored tree of life pattern covers almost every surface of this bedroom and is only broken up by the muted checks which line the curtains and the bed hangings.** Below **An armchair uses the same combination of patterns, with the tree of life on the front and the checks on the back.**

Tartan plaid is another variety of checked fabric. It owes much of its appealingly romantic image to the Victorian love of Sir Walter Scott's novels, coupled with their queen's deep attachment to the Highlands. The passionate delight taken by both Queen Victoria and Prince Albert in all things Scottish led to them decorating some of their rooms at Balmoral in plaid. Even the floors were laid with tartan carpets. These rooms were to have a huge influence on the taste of the day, eventually leading to plaid's widespread popularity as an upholstery fabric, in spite of the fact that it was originally used only for clothing.

The Victorian passion for rich colors manifested itself in the production of tartans using the new aniline dyes. These tartans

Left and right **A wool tartan plaid has been hung on the walls of this guest room at Glamis Castle in Scotland. The soft greens and blues are a reminder of the pines and heathers outside.**
Far right **The curtains and dust ruffle are made from the same tartan fabric and help to create a uniform look.**

rejoiced in a tumultuous riot of unconventional color and were unlike the softly muted tones of the early tartans. The latter were woven with yarns colored by natural dyes indigenous to the area, resulting in mellow hues which echoed the highland moors of their origins.

The deep, rich colors much in demand during this era, which we now think of as characteristic of tartan, and its simple linear patterns, make it a popular choice for creating a warm comforting atmosphere. Naturally, plaid is a popular fabric in Scotland, where it is used for curtains and upholstery in every type of room. It is also used for wall hangings, which act as insulators during the winter. You will find tartan in the United States and French interiors as well. The rectilinear patterns make it particularly suitable for upholstery on plain, squarish furniture, such as solid-looking armchairs and sofas, or a small plaid footstool could be just what is needed to boost a room's decorative scheme.

India is the source of another hugely popular checked fabric, madras. The term "madras" was coined by 19th century plantation workers in the West Indies to describe the brightly colored cotton squares imported from the eponymous southern Indian city and worn as headscarves. Today the term tends to be associated with a lightweight, somewhat randomly checked cloth woven in a huge variety of vivid hues.

The lightweight, rich colors and relatively low cost of madras cottons lend themselves to all sorts of dramatic design effects. The bright hues of this material tend not to be colorfast, so they are best used in dark corners with little or no direct light, or they will fade over time. Due to its lightweight qualities, madras can be pinched and pleated with ease,

Top and left **A colorful madras cotton used on a rigidly shaped sofa in a formal setting helps to add a note of casual informality.**
Right **The most common use for madras is in tableware, and the vibrant colors of this tablecloth and matching napkin brighten up any dinner setting.**

wound in generous swags around poles or draped in elaborate swathes. Mix a swag of madras lengths together for an exotic look. If you are looking for a uniform arrangement in your checks, however, remember that one of the idiosyncrasies of madras is that the pattern is not woven in a regular fashion, so a double stripe or a forgotten repeat is quite likely to occur. For this reason, avoid using the fabric where perfect matching of adjoining lengths is crucial, for instance on furniture covers. If madras is being used to make curtains, it should always be interlined unless a thin, wispy effect is desired.

Checks can be mixed with each other or with other patterns in an almost infinite number of combinations, as the photographs in this chapter demonstrate. But the most important rule to remember is that, with checks, there are no rules. Whether you decide to use large checks, small, discreetly neutral colors or even vibrant rainbow hues, the lure of the check will never wane.

When decorators use the term **motif**, they are usually describing a series of repeated themed patterns. Motifs can be small or large scale, picked out in a single color, or emblazoned across a rug or upholstery fabric in a bright multitude of hues.

motif

THE VARIETY OF METHODS OF PRESENTING MOTIFS ARE ALMOST LIMITLESS: THEY CAN BE WOVEN OR PRINTED ONTO UPHOLSTERY FABRIC, PAINTED FREESTYLE OR STENCILED ONTO WALLS AND FLOORS, APPLIQUÉD, EMBROIDERED, ENGRAVED, ETCHED, STAMPED, TOOLED, CARVED, OR CAST. Broadly speaking, motifs can be scaled to suit any interior and divided into two categories, figurative or representational. The first category is mainly made up of geometrically based forms and include the Greek key, polka dots, lozenges, and Vitruvian scrolls. Representational motifs are usually inspired by animals, plants and manmade objects, and often have a symbolic meaning. Shells, flowers, cherubs, and *fleur de lys*—whose form was derived in the Middle Ages from irises and whose name is a corruption of *fleur de louis*, named after France's King, Louis VII—are all examples of this motif.

Above **A modern interpretation of a paisley pattern is used to make a cover for a cushion.**
Left **In a modern interior in Italy, the walls have been painted in a series of concentric squares and a lampshade has been given a decorative border of Vitruvian scrolls all around its base.**

The great appeal of motifs is their flexibility, which makes it easy to incorporate them into virtually any kind of decorative scheme and in any environment. They look equally at home in a Manhattan loft conversion, a 1930s duplex, an old clapboard cottage, or an Irish castle. They can be used in an almost infinite variety of ways: to form a border around the walls, to decorate lampshades, bedspreads, curtains, or repeated, seemingly at random, in a series of kitchen tiles; the possibilities are seemingly endless. A motif can also be used to add decoration in a single form: a large appliqué star, for instance, could be emblazoned across a pillow, or a door handle made from shell-shaped resin . More frequently, however, motifs are used as a recurring theme, unifying a room with a pattern that echoes across the walls and upholstery, and re-emerging in such accessories as pillows, and wastepaper baskets.

Small motifs are often used *en masse* across large surface areas to give the effect of a large-scale pattern when viewed from a distance. When examined closely, such patterns reveal themselves to be composed of repeating motifs in varying sizes, artfully arranged in such a way that a highly decorative design is created. William Morris, the much-acclaimed 19th-century designer, used this form of illusion to good effect in many of the wallpapers and fabrics he designed.

The use of motifs in decorating is governed by traditions that have evolved over the centuries, and although many designs are copied from such traditions it is always worth remembering that there are no formal rules to the use of motif patterns as decoration.

One of the most frequently used motifs, down the centuries and across the globe, is the star. This geometrically inspired pattern, frequently designed in highly stylized forms, can vary greatly in size and outline, some stars having four points, others five, six, or even more. It is not too farfetched to claim that stars really do have a twinkling quality and have often been imbued with great religious and cultural significance. A decorative pattern composed of stars is both refreshing and light-hearted, the jaunty, clean-cut lines of the stars providing visual appeal.

Far right The dining room of a summer beach house. The only form of pattern that appears is a pretty star motif, but it is all the more distinctive for that. The dining chairs are slipcovered using inexpensive cotton. To jazz up the plain color and echo the proximity to the sea, a single star—almost a starfish in fact—is appliquéd to each chair back.
Above right The star motif is repeated in the border down the sides and along the bottom of the curtains and is also just visible as a subtle pattern stenciled around the edge of the wooden floor.
Right A chair seat is livened up with a circle of stenciled stars in a color to match the paintwork on the chair frame.

The Islamic world can fairly be described as the spiritual home of the star-as-motif. Prohibited by their religion from depicting any living form, Islamic artists found that the star's linear qualities made it a perfect decorative device for homes and mosques alike. The star motif occurs frequently in the geometric tiling which is an essential feature of Islamic architecture since as far back as the 10th century. They are especially popular in places of learning and worship. Very often the stars are not immediately obvious as they are indirectly formed as a result of other repeating patterns, and it is only when they are looked at from a distance that a strongly geometric pattern of stars can be discerned.

roman shade with decorative swirls

With the growth in popularity of minimalist interiors, long heavy curtains so much in vogue during the Eighties are giving way to simpler window treatments. Shades of all sorts are a useful way of gaining both the required privacy and a desirable decorative finish. Pleated roman shades, in particular, work well with a simpler style of interior.

Materials and equipment

fabric for the shade (see step 1 for amount)

lining fabric (see steps 6 and 7 for amount)

1½-inch wide trim, approximately wide for two long sides and bottom of shade

narrow trim, approximately ¾ inch wide for two long sides and bottom of shade

narrow trim to make the swirl pattern, approximately double the length of the plain trims

cardboard for swirl template

tailor's chalk

scissors or craft knife

1-inch wide velcro, to fit the width of the shade

1 x 1-inch wooden strip to fit the window

cord, eyes, and rings

wall cleat

Preparing the shade

1 Roman shades can either hang outside the window frame so that the entire frame is covered or they can fit neatly into a recess. Measure the width and length of the window in order to calculate the amount of fabric you will need. Cut enough fabric for your shade plus an allowance of 1 inch for each of the side hems and 1½ inches for the top and bottom hems. Fold and press these allowances to the wrong side and then open out again to mark the finished line.

Making a template for the swirl design

2 Trace or copy the repeat and corner pattern (see right). Scale them up to a suitable size on a photocopier—bear in mind that the scale of the swirls should be of the right size to repeat complete swirl patterns along the bottom of the shade. Trace the swirls on the cardboard, making them ¼ inch wide, and cut them out with a craft knife.

Sewing the trim and swirls to the shade

3 Pin the wide trim to the sides and bottom of the shade 2½ inches from the side raw

edges, and 3¼ inches from the bottom raw edge, mitering the bottom corners. (When the raw edges have been turned in, your trim should sit 1½ inches from the outside edges of the shade.) Pin, baste, and topstitch to the shade. Next, place the narrow trim 1½ inches from the wide trim. Pin, baste, and topstitch to the shade as for the wide trim.

4 Use your template and tailor's chalk to mark the position of the swirl design all the way along the bottom and down each side of the shade. As the design needs to fit neatly across the bottom of the shade, start with the corner swirls. Once you have positioned these correctly, work your way across the bottom of the shade and up the sides. Like the wide and narrow trims, the swirls "disappear" into the top of the shade. The templates should be placed so as to leave a 2-inch gap between the narrow trim and the bottom edge of the swirl design.

5 Pin the swirl trim over the chalk marks. Baste, and top stitch in place.

Preparing the lining

6 Cut out a piece of lining fabric the same length as the main fabric, plus an extra ¼ inch per pleat added onto the length (to calculate the number of pleats, see step 7 below) and 1 inch narrower than the finished shade measurement.

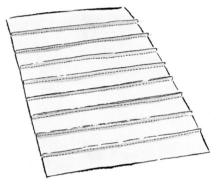

7 From the top, mark the pleat lines about 16 inches apart, but make sure you leave enough material hanging at the bottom of the shade so that the last pleat sits just above the swirl pattern along the bottom edge. Form ⅛-inch wide folds along the line of each pleat and machine stitch them about ⅛ inch from the edge of the fold to form parallel casings that will serve as anchor points for attaching the rings.

Attaching the lining

8 With right sides together, pin, baste, and machine stitch the main fabric to the lining along the side edges, leaving a ⅝-inch seam allowance. Press the seams open and turn the shade to the right side. With the lined side facing, pin the fabric together at the top

and bottom and press the pieces flat, along the edges pressed in step 1, leaving an equal margin down each side. Along the bottom edge, working with both fabrics, turn up a 1½ inch hem, then neatly fold the corners into miters and slipstitch by hand in place.

Putting up the shade

9 At the top, turn in ½ inch and attach the furry side of the velcro. Use a staple gun or tacks to secure the hooked side of the velcro to the top of the wooden strip.

10 Handsew the shade rings to the casing on the lining, spacing them roughly 12 inches apart across the width of the shade.

11 Screw the eyes into the bottom of the wooden strips at points which correspond exactly with the position of the rings sewn onto the casings made across the lining. Secure the strips to the window frame.

12 Lay the shade face down on a large flat surface. Knot the cords to the bottom ring of each row of rings and loop through so the cords run vertically from the bottom of the shade to the top. Once the cords have been threaded through the top ring, run them through the eyes from left to right and knot them together at the side. Make sure there is plenty of extra cord left over to hang down the side of the shade.

13 Attach the velcro at the top of the shade to the velcro on the wooden strip to secure the shade to the window frame. Screw the cleat to the right-hand side of the window frame to wrap the cord around when the shade is pulled up.

Bold swirls add a distinctive border to an otherwise plain roman shade and also outline the outer edge of the window frame once they have been pulled down.

This page **An exquisite mosaic floor is an ideal choice in a spacious hall and provides the cue for the wall decoration. The star motif has been lifted from the floor design and translated into bold repeats. The large-scale stars are handpainted, forming a lattice pattern. Although a daring step, the stars do not overpower because soft-hued paint has been used. The dramatic and unusual ceiling light also picks up the celestial theme.**

Over the centuries, carpets have repeatedly incorporated stars as a motif. Inspiration was often derived from the "Crivelli" star (named after the 15th-century Venetian painter, Carlo Crivelli, who depicted starred carpets in his paintings) and is to be found on a variety of Turkish, Caucasian, and Spanish weavings dating from the 15th century. The densely patterned carpets beloved by the Victorians are too busy for most modern eyes, and so today's patterned carpets are far more likely to be decorated with a repeating pattern of simple stars or a gothic trefoil.

Stars are an appropriate choice of motif for either a bedroom or a bathroom, both rooms where one

Left **The star motif repeated on the walls in the entrance hall opposite is echoed above these double doors. The full star has now become a half star to fit the space above the doorway. The straight lines of the half star are softened by symmetrical panels showing a bordered Vitruvian scroll pattern, and the scrolls are picked up again in the lampshades and appliquéd as a border on the window shade in the room opposite.**

This page **You do not need to stick to one type of motif in a room; mix and match them to good effect. Here dark wood antique furniture is given a colorful, jazzy lift with a floral scroll pattern and slim checked bolsters and a fun, star-shaped pillow. This exuberant mix of patterns works well because of the strong unifying color scheme.**

has the opportunity to lay back and gaze heavenward. Stars are such simple shapes that they can be painted freestyle or stenciled onto a surface. Depending on the room in question and the overall decorative scheme, a galaxy of stars is not always necessary. In most cases, a handful or even a couple of carefully placed stars will suffice. Try using them to dress up a plain cotton loose cover by stenciling or appliquéing a star to its back, giving a sophisticated twist to an otherwise nondescript chair. A border of stars around a cushion or on a pair of curtains with tiebacks to match, a border of little tiny stars around the seat of an upholstered wooden-framed occasional chair, or a pelmet or bed corona decorated with a line of painted stars; these are all ways of brightening up a room with a minimum of effort. Large-scale stars, simply outlined in paint, are

Above **Mosaic floors are most suitable for entrance halls and circulation spaces since they are robust and make a statement of grandeur. Here an intricate mosaic floor made of hexagons is bordered with Vitruvian scrolls—originally a Greek form of ornamentation.**
Right **A bleached wooden floor is stenciled in a diagonal check of pale tones and each adjoining corner has been given a darker dot.**
Far right **Various floor patterns to draw the eye. Wood floors can be jazzed up with hard-drying paint and lacquer, and the blandness of sisal rugs can easily be lifted by using dots, stars, and borders such as the series of interlocking circles shown here. (See also the project on pages 130–131.)**

a marvelous way of decorating awkward areas of a house like staircases and landings. Painting them in outline rather than filling them in as a solid block of color actually increases the overall visual impact of the finished motif.

On the whole, more attention is given to choosing upholstery fabrics, window or wall treatments, and even to selecting the right accessories than to deciding on how to make the most of the floor area. This is a pity since the options are virtually endless and a poorly coordinated floor can ruin

the overall effect of even the most stylish of rooms. Strong decorative statements can be made by painting a motif across a wooden floor. Used outside on wooden decks or even inside on ordinary wooden floorboards stenciling is a marvelous way of creating pattern and interest underfoot. Yet another type of flooring that has now become increasingly popular is natural sisal or coir matting. Although attractive in its own right, the pale straw colors and subtle textural

quality of these coverings can be transformed with a unique and unusual floor decoration with the addition of a painted or stenciled border, using the motif of your choice. Stencils are a brilliant way of introducing motifs and can be used to create anything from a charmingly naive look to a more sophisticated elaborate design. Do not then detract from the effect by going for very elaborate furnishings, unless you want to create a rather cluttered look, as such environments tend not to be

greek key border

Stenciling a carpet or rug is a simple and inexpensive way of adding decoration to an otherwise plain piece of floor covering. The Greek key pattern, with its strong horizontal and vertical lines, works best in bold colors and is particularly suited to contemporary tastes. Here it has been added to sisal carpeting which is very hard wearing, and used as a rug this material can help to soften the appearance of hard granite floors. The floral motif repeated across the rug, as shown in the photograph opposite, is an optional addition which could help to break up a particularly large floor space.

Materials and equipment

10 sheets of stiff stencil board

tracing paper

carbon paper

tape measure

scalpel or craft knife

metal or wooden ruler

masking tape

stencil brush

rag

dark stencil paint

Planning the layout

1 As with any form of stenciling or freestyle decorative painting, the battle is won in the planning stages. Great care needs to be paid to the placement and scale of the design if it is to succeed.

Make a scaled-down plan on paper of your design, before cutting your stencils, paying special attention to the number of repeats necessary and the corners. Complicated as it sounds, you are better off doing it this way, since the Greek key pattern is not very adaptable and you will have to stick to the precise set of measurements and number of repeats you have worked out on your plan for the project to resolve itself correctly.

The original rug on which this project is based measures 33 x 50 feet and has a contrasting border. If you choose a different-sized rug, you can scale your stencil up or down according to its dimensions.

The corner squares need two stencils, one for the outer square and one for the inner square. The exact size of the corner pattern could vary according to the dimensions of your rug, this one is 5½ inches square around the outside edge, with the borders measuring ¾ inch across. The Greek key itself is 5½ inches wide and 11 inches long. Based on these figures the rug has 10 repeats along the narrow sides and 16 repeats down each long side. Scale the template up or down according to the dimensions of your particular rug. The stencil for the key needs to be cut out of the stiffest stencil board you

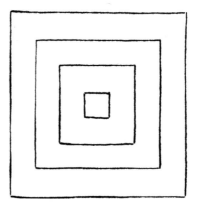

can buy, otherwise, the inner projections may bend during painting, resulting in a smudged and distorted pattern.

There should be a gap of approximately ¾ inch between the corner squares and the start of the Greek key stencil repeats, but this can be adjusted to allow you to fit an exact number of repeats of the Greek key pattern along each side.

Preparing the stencil

2 Trace the two designs (the main Greek key design and the corner square). Scale them up on a photocopier to fit your chosen dimensions. Using carbon paper, transfer each design onto two pieces of stencil board, making sure that you leave a border of 1¼ inches around each side of the corner squares; 1¼ inches on the long side of the key pattern and ¾ inch on the short side. Using a scalpel or a craft knife, carefully cut out each design. Make two stencils of the Greek key so you can alternate them as they become wet with paint.

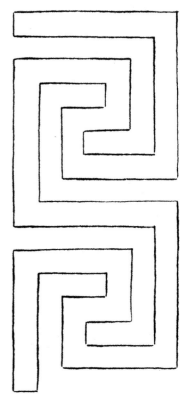

Stenciling

3 Start by painting in the four corners. Align edges of the outer square stencil against the border of the rug and anchor with masking tape. Stick masking tape to the back of the inner square stencil and position it in the center of the outer square. Dip the stencil brush into the dark paint and brush off the excess with a rag. Gently tap the brush across the stencils until you achieve complete coverage. Repeat at the other three corners of the rug.

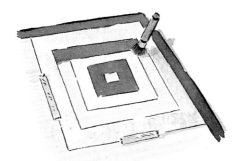

4 Once all the squares are dry, you can start on the Greek key design. Align the side of your Greek key stencil with the inner edge of the rug's border and align the top with the outer outer edge of the corner square; anchor with masking tape. Dab on dark paint, using the same technique you employed with the corner squares. When the paint has dried, carefully peel away the stencil board. Reposition it by overlaying the top column of the first key against the painted "tail" of the last key and carefully align it with the border of the rug.

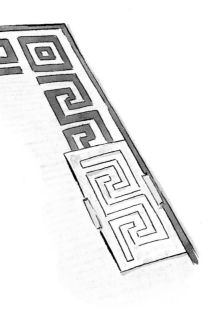

Repeat until you have stenciled the Greek key pattern all the way around the rug. When you reach the last key along a line of repeats, mask off the "tail" of the last key to make a neat finish on the series of repeats.

The angular pattern of the Greek key pattern is balanced by the evenly spaced flower motifs that appear across the rug.

very restful to live with. There is a long tradition of animals being used as motifs, on clothing or furnishings. Think of medieval knights riding into battle wearing their crest, such as an eagle, lion, pelican, or boar's head, as a distinguishing badge atop their helmets. European aristocracy has used these crests as a means of decorating their homes and the treasures inside them for many centuries now. Contemporary fabric companies now carry lines clearly inspired by heraldic crests as this has become quite popular today. They range from traditional designs to intriguingly offbeat renditions such as the whimsical animal prints of Celia Birtwell, a British fabric designer.

Bees are a motif that is inextricably linked with the Regency period, due to Napoleon Bonaparte adopting the bee as his personal emblem. Metal bees had been found at the excavation of the tomb of Chilperic I, a 6th-century Frankish king and hero, and Napoleon valued this link, however tenuous, with the early rulers of France. The Imperial household had bees woven into textiles for hangings, tapestries, upholstery, and robes, and applied in ormolu to furniture. Napoleon III retained the emblem, and to this day bees ornament the chimney pieces of the Chateau de Pierrefonds, which he actually had restored for use as a royal palace. A Napoleonic-style silk fabric woven

with a pattern of bees is the perfect choice for upholstering formal Regency furniture, chaise longues, sofas and neoclassical dining chairs. It also looks great used on pillows, especially the bolster shape which was so popular in Europe and the United States in the early 19th century.

This page **The wallpaper in this dining room shows a random leaf motif. The background shade is the sort of brown we see on brown paper bags. The pattern is also painted over the radiator cover to disguise it and to give a feeling of continuity to the whole room. Collections of white pebbles are arranged along the top of the radiator and on the mantelpiece to echo the floating leaves.**

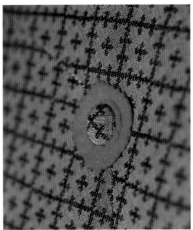

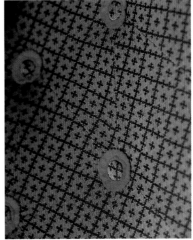

Above **The decorative buttoning on the wing chair is shown in detail. Small circles of fabric are cut out and laid behind each of the individual buttons to give them added emphasis.**

Left **An** eclectic mixture of motifs, patterns, and textures can be seen in the living room of this apartment. The wing chair is upholstered in a geometric weave and stands on a lovely flat-weave patterned floor rug.

Bees are powerful symbols of industry and order, which helps to explain their widespread popularity during the Victorian era. The worker bee became an emblem of the 19th-century self-help groups and can be seen across the mosaic floor of Alfred Waterhouse's great Manchester Town Hall, a glorious monument to Victorian civic pride.

Birds are an ancient form of motif and were particularly widespread during the Middle Ages, a period when falconry and hawking were popular activities. In the 18th century, the increasing availability of illustrated natural history books were a particular inspiration to a multitude of

designers and craftsmen, leading to avian appearances in the most unlikely decorative locations. Stylized birds could be seen adorning plasterwork, ceramics, and embroideries. The ho-ho bird, a mythical phoenix-like creature, has to be one of the most splendidly named birds ever to be used as a motif. Its popularity was at its height in the middle of the 18th century, when it fluttered about adorning a multitude of chinoiserie-inspired decorative schemes.

The lion is frequently found as a decorative element, and in its incarnation as king of the beasts, it symbolizes strength, courage, pride, fortitude, and majesty. For this reason, it is often found allied to ceremonial furnishings.

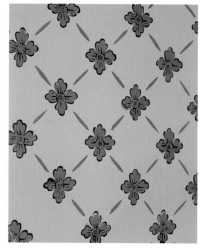

Left Inspirational stenciling is on show to the public at Karl von Linné's charming rural museum in Sweden. Simple repeating motifs are painted close together so that they form a dense pattern above the dado rail.

Above A much more complicated stencil design is detailed here.

Right This intricate, lacy stencil has been done in charcoal black and painted on wooden boards under a flight of stairs, adding a hidden touch of decoration.

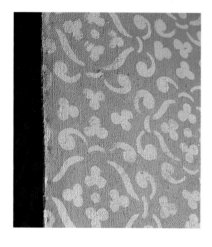

This page **A feast of stencils is on display at Gripsholm Castle in Sweden.** The walls and ceilings are paneled in wood and intricately painted and stenciled in repeating patterns. The overall impression is one of a wonderful medley of colors and designs.

Opposite **A deeply recessed window incorporates benches in the paneling, with a stencil on a dark background above.**

Far right **Meeting ceiling panels.**

Textile design has always made extensive use of plant motifs, especially floral subjects. These days, however, people tend to think of floral fabrics as being synonymous with flower-strewn chintzes, an association many of us find rather worrying. If you like the idea of living surrounded by plants but are put off by the prettiness of floral patterns, you can find plenty of less fussy patterns in fabrics inspired by antique botanical prints. Some look as if an 18th-century print room of botanicals has been literally transferred onto cloth. This type of material works wonderfully well if used for curtains, slipcovers, and cushions

in a room such as a living room or library. It also lends itself well to being gathered or knife-pleated to the back of either glazed or wire mesh cupboard doors. This is a good way of using fabric patterned with motifs, as it breaks up the visual mass of a piece of furniture that would otherwise be too bulky or dominating.

Motifs inspired by flowers look great in a bedroom, particularly if they are used as a cocoon-like wall covering, or to upholster a bed's headboard and valance, finishing the room off with matching curtains. Floral motifs are, in general, a particularly attractive and cozy way of decorating small

bedrooms such as in cramped urban apartments, as they add a breath of fresh air and remind one of the countryside with their natural forms and colors.

The strong graphic quality of the leaf explains its popularity as a motif down the centuries. acanthus, ivy, oak, palm, thistle, and laurel are just a few of the types of leaves to be encountered in a variety of interiors, adorning large surfaces and their associated fixtures and fittings throughout the history of decorating. Foliage was an important strand of the Art Nouveau movement. Leaves, stylized as flowing tendrils, can be seen decorating all manner of

This page **Small repeating floral patterns are popular the world over. They are extremely useful: not only are they pretty, but they act as a perfect foil for larger patterns, and they mask dust and dirt.**
Above and right **A traditional French bed has head- and footboards that have been upholstered in a woven floral brocade.**
Above middle **A stripe with a small repeating motif.**
Above left **A woven floral motif.**

Below Inside a beautiful chateau in **Provence in southern France,** the study is done up with pretty silk brocades. Brocade is a rich woven fabric with a flat background which is silky to the touch. In addition to the delicate floral designs on display, there is plenty of texture in this interior as the brocade has an all-over raised design.

Far right Floral motifs with undulating verticals are a good choice of pattern for curtains, giving them movement and grace.

surfaces from carpets and fireplaces to porcelain and silver vessels. Acorns are a motif in their own right and like the pomegranate, another fruit which has inspired motifs through the ages, are linked symbolically to concepts of life, fecundity and immortality. Easily turned on a lathe, the acorn has the perfect shape to crown a wooden finial.

Robert Adam, the great 18th-century architect and designer, often used to echo the ceiling design of a room in its carpet. Very few people live in such grand surroundings these days, but on a lesser scale, it is possible to be inspired by Adam's example and take a motif used elsewhere in the room, for instance a floral sprig from the upholstery fabric of a chair, and to repeat it elsewhere in the room, which helps to draw disparate elements together.

A repeating ornament of interlacing ribbons, known as guilloche, sometimes forms circles enriched by rosettes or other flower forms. Chiswick House, a

Above **The decorative garland motif is used to follow the lines of the paneling, running up the side of the open doorway.**
Left **An 18th-century bedroom in a French chateau has paneled walls. A pretty, formal garland is painted around a portrait, (see also the project on pages 142–143). The chair is upholstered in silk brocade.**
Far left **The tree of life pattern exists in many forms; here is a stylized version of it painted all over the walls of an 18th-century chateau in Normandy, northern France. The china blues give a fresh, classical look.**

garlanded painted panel

This charming 18th-century bedroom in a Normandy chateau has panels which frame entwined garlands of ribbons and foliage. Paneled walls were a classic 17th- and 18th-century architectural and interior feature, especially in Europe, Scandinavia, and the U.S. If your house does not have paneled walls, you could create *faux* paneling with wooden molding and paint garlands within the panels as shown here. The garland can be painted within existing paneling or can be used alone to create a paneled effect.

soft pencil

ruler

tracing paper

carbon paper

stencil board for bow template

scalpel or craft knife

low-tack painter's tape

latex paint for walls

wide paintbrush for painting walls

flat acrylic paint in 3 colors—a gray-blue for the bow and ribbon, white to mix for the highlights, and forest green for the garland and leaves

stencil brush

¾-inch wide paintbrush

⅜-inch wide paintbrush

stencil brush

rag

fine-tip artist's brush

Preparation

1 Make sure the walls are clean and dry. Paint them, if necessary, with two coats of latex in a neutral background color. Let it dry thoroughly.

Planning the layout

2 The scale of your garland will depend entirely on the size of the room, the height of the ceiling, the size of the existing panels and the size of the painting you wish to frame. Taking all these factors into account, lightly pencil in a ¾-inch wide ribbon, indenting the top corners as shown below.

Preparing the bow stencil

3 Trace the pattern shown right, then enlarge it to the desired proportions on a photocopier. Using carbon paper, transfer the design to the stencil board and cut out carefully around the outline, using a scalpel or a craft knife.

Painting the ribbon

4 Using the gray-blue paint and a ¾-inch paintbrush, carefully paint in the ribbon border. Let it dry thoroughly before you proceed with the next stage of painting. Mix the white paint with the gray-blue paint in a ratio of three parts white to one part color. Now use the ⅜-inch paintbrush to dab long streaks of the resulting color along the middle of the ribbon; this particular technique is used to create highlights all the way around the painted frame.

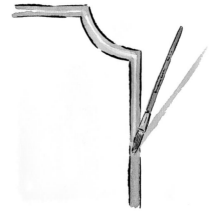

Stenciling

5 Figure out the exact top center of the ribbon and place the bow stencil over it. Anchor it in place with tape. Dip the stencil brush in the gray-blue paint and brush off the excess with a rag. Gently tap the brush across the stencil. Use the paint very sparingly and go over the area a few times rather than saturating the brush with paint. Let it dry thoroughly. Use the ⅜-inch brush and the blended paint to dab more highlights along the bow.

Planning and painting the garland

6 Based on the illustration below, lightly pencil in the swags of the garland, starting and ending it in the center of the stenciled bow. Remember as you are doing so, that the garland weaves around the ribbon, and you will need to make its outline pass alternately behind and in front of the ribbon to achieve this effect.

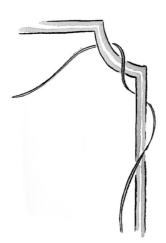

Using a fine artist's brush and forest green paint, paint in the garland's outline freestyle. Try to make the line as smooth and continuous as possible, lifting the brush only as the garland passes behind the painted frame. Let it dry thoroughly.

In this project we have decorated the garland with leaf forms, however, there are many other decorative effects and motifs that can be added to the garland instead, such as floral sprigs, berries, ferns, and fruits.

Painting the leaves

7 Based on the leaf forms illustrated below, lightly pencil in the outlines of the leaves all the way around the garlanded frame, varying the size and shape of each leaf slightly as you go. Using the fine artist's brush and the green paint, paint in each leaf freestyle.

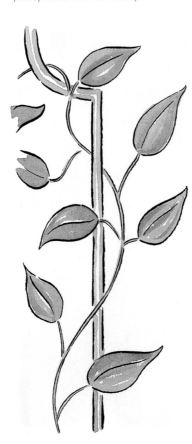

A combination of stenciling and freestyle painting gives a touch of decorative grandeur to a plain paneled bedroom wall.

famous Palladian villa in west London, boasts a double guilloche wall molding, but curiously, the double width waters down the impact of the pattern. A single band makes a bolder statement, and this definition makes it appear highly sophisticated. A stunning overall effect can be achieved by combining a couple of plain striped borders, one wider than the other, acting as a curb on the swirls of the guilloche. A guilloche border of this type is very effective used as an outline decorating a plain cardboard lampshade, or it can be used to paint in panels to break up an expanse of wall, or screen-printed as a border it can be added on to a pair of curtains or around a duvet cover in an otherwise plain color.

The Greek key pattern is another popular motif that has survived since antiquity. A classic motif with interlocking right-angled and vertical lines, it is sometimes broken up into its component elements, but is more often applied as a continuous pattern. A common variation is achieved by doubling the lines

Above **An unusual woven silk is used on an elegant sofa.**

Right **Silk damask pillows work well against the rich sofa fabric.**

Left and far left **Classical patterned silhouette wallpaper is used in both a bathroom and a small hallway. The chair placed in the hall has been upholstered in woven striped linen in complementary shades. In the bathroom is a richly patterned tiled floor, typical of the kind seen throughout France.**

Above and right **Provençal prints**
have long been popular in their
native France, but their appeal is
widespread, and they are now available in every imaginable
variety, as fabrics, wallpapers, and
all kinds of accessories, from lampshades and scatter cushions to
bedspreads and bolsters. In a small
guest bedroom, the walls are
papered in a fresh blue and white
Provençal print. The headboards
have been upholstered in a
complementary stripe and the
duvet covers in a small check.
Far right **A more intricate golden
Provençal** print dresses the
window of a bedroom, where the
sunlight brings out the richness of
the color, and highlights the
detailed motif pattern and the
gentle frills at the side.

of the key to produce an effect of perspective. The Greek key reached a crescendo of popularity during the vogue for all things classical during the neoclassical and Regency periods between the middle of the 18th and 19th centuries. Popular in many guises, it functions well as a decorative motif for cast-iron balconies, painted onto porcelain as a frieze, as an architectural molding, or painted onto walls as a decorative substitute for a dado rail. A truly modern interpretation is to paint a Greek key on a sisal rug as a decorative border (see the project on pages 130–131), it is particularly effective for sisal when used as a stair runner. The Greek key has appeared in many different permutations over the generations and as yet shows no sign of waning in popularity.

Possibly the simplest of the geometric motifs is the simple dot. Frequently ignored as a theme for interior decoration, it has been hugely popular over the years as an element in fashionable clothing. In the 1950s, when the polka dot was at the height of its popularity, there was a brief vogue

Above, and above left **On a sunny deck with a sea view, a North American coverlet woven on a multishaft loom catches the sunlight. Its distinctive patterning and heavy-weight texture make it an ideal throw for use in an out-door area such as this.**
Above right **In a wide open porch-way a wooden bench is draped with an American country quilt.**
Right **A detail of the fern-like motif on the country quilt shows that it has been attached using an appliqué technique.**
Far right **A magnificent overscaled tree of life motif woven in linen in strong colors is all the pattern that is needed in an otherwise unadorned country bedroom.**

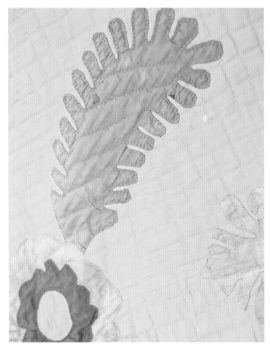

for spotted china. It is a curious fact that such a simple and happy motif is not more popular. Spotted fabric would make lovely cheery shades or curtains in a child's bedroom, and would brighten up a somber kitchen. In more formal rooms, spotted material made up into skirted or smocked lampshades, trimmed with a contrasting bobble fringe, would be a witty and effective way of using dots as a motif. Painted dots used in conjunction with other simple patterns, say a couple of wavy horizontal lines in contrasting colors, can be used to create a delightfully artistic substitute for a cornice. Another idea is to break up a wall surface by painting it one color up to dado level

and then to paint a frieze of dots the same color slightly above, presenting an interesting alternative to a conventional dado molding. Dots offer enormous decorative potential just waiting to be explored.

Unlike the English, who are only too happy to sink back into a squashy sofa, the French, by nature, tend toward a more formal style of interiors where motif-patterned fabrics

Above **Printed paisley is now available from many fabric suppliers as both upholstery and curtain materials. Here it is seen sewn up into a long square bench pillow.**
Middle **An antique paisley shawl sits neatly on a chair.**
Right **A pair of Roman shades are made from a modern printed paisley in a striped formation.**

provide the only note of frivolity. The French love to use the delicately scaled floral motifs which seem to be an essential ingredient in the most sophisticated of their interiors. The most stylish of these are woven in silk and have a delicate feminine quality. Often the motifs are formed from simple flowered sprigs, and yet others are formed by combining these sprigs with thin lines in a matching or contrasting

color, and the most complex are set into a trellised framework giving an impression of geometric regularity. The latter types of floral patterns are well suited to the regular outlines of the wooden-framed furniture beloved by the French. Floral motif patterned material is also a favourite choice for wall coverings in France, although it is usually only used above the dado

rail, which will avoid swamping the room in a thicket of stylized flowers.

Provençal prints are instantly recognizable because of the intensity of their colors and the brilliant use of little floral and geometric motifs. These bold, busy fabrics are so closely linked with the provençal ethos that it seems incredible to realize that, in common with many other patterned fabrics, their origins are to be found in India. When the first shipments of painted cloths arrived in Marseilles in the late 16th century, they were known as indiennes. It was not long before they were being reproduced in the southern city of Marseilles, where they were printed using hand-carved blocks of wood. A host of cottage

studios sprung up, each with its own distinctive motif patterns and vibrantly colored dyes. Today the homespun quality may have been swamped by the 20th century's wave of industrialization, but the fabrics are still being produced and have enjoyed a renaissance in popularity over the last couple of decades. Provençal prints are traditionally found in the kitchens and bathrooms of farmhouses, but they work equally well in these rooms in an urban environment, bringing with them a welcome splash of country color and with that a breath of fresh air. Their intense hues and bold motifs make it hard to combine them with other patterns, but you shouldn't

Left An antique bed is made up with fine white bedlinen and antique wool paisley shawls. Paisley was originally an Indian motif which may have been inspired by the form of a pine cone or a tear drop. Paisley shawls that were produced in the Himalayan hinterland of Kashmir were originally worn by men as luxurious shoulder wraps against cold weather. In the 19th century, they were produced in vast quantities in the Scottish town of Paisley.

be afraid of using them in formal settings where they work particularly well when used in conjunction with plain weaves, which provide a suitably neutral background for them.

Much of the design and artistic inspiration of the 20th century has been derived from ethnic motifs and symbols. Ethnic textiles are a wonderful way of introducing a dash of exoticism and individuality to any interior, and their patterning is often surprisingly sophisticated. They are almost always made using bright and vibrant colors as well, so you will have to think about how they will fit in with your furnishings. But do not be afraid to embark on a decorative adventure and incorporate ethnic patterns into your home. Top taste-brokers Christopher Gibbs and David Mlinaric take great delight in mixing ethnic objects and textiles with more conventional western elements and have built an international reputation on the basis of the stunning results.

Just as many of the most influential artists of the early 20th century sought inspiration from the art and sculpture of Africa, textile designers today often seek inspiration from a rich variety of ethnic traditions. The cut-pile raffia textiles produced by the Kuba of Zaire are a good example of the graphic and intricate qualities of the geometric designs traditionally produced on the African continent. There is a delightful anecdote about the Kuba people which tells how, when presented with a motorcycle in the 1920s, their king was unmoved by the machine itself, but fascinated by the tire marks which it left in the sand. The pattern was promptly added to the Kuba repertoire of motifs.

The graphic sophistication of many of these African designs is such that they do not look out of place framed and hung on the walls of a contemporary-style apartment. Despite the boldness of these designs they are unpretentious and the definite lines have a pleasing clarity about them. Although they can tend to overwhelm when used in large quantities, picking out certain details and accessories in a room with these fabrics set against a neutral background can look very stylish.

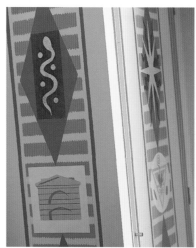

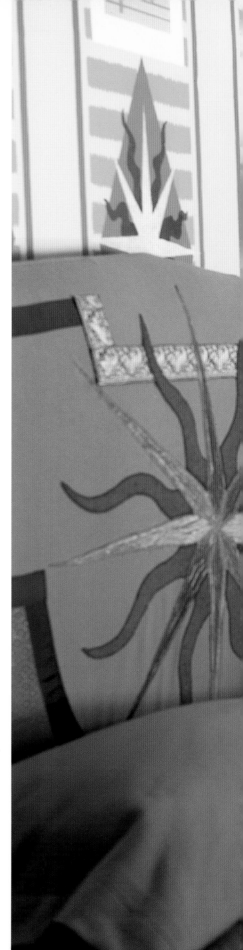

Both pages **A tiny loft bedroom is decked with high-impact motifs by a contemporary designer. The room has a tribal flavor to it with the panels resembling African shields; you can pick out stars and snakes among other more symbolic motifs. The bed has a matching bedspread and headboard, both of which have been decorated with a large appliquéd tendriled star to create a dramatic effect.**

Many Indian saris rely on motifs of one kind or another for their pattern. They are a fabulous source of relatively inexpensive and unusual fabrics. Saris can be made into cushion pillows, shades, draped over tables or stunning pelmets, creating a really individual window treatment. A simple cotton sari looks great used as a canopy over a bath tub; the sari is suspended high up on the wall and drapes elegantly over a pair of large wooden bosses mounted on the walls over the bath in a triangular configuration. To complete the scheme, add a matching shade.

If you are of an artistic inclination, try inventing your own personal motif and creating a really unique interior. If no pattern

Opposite **This sofa arrangement demonstrates that the possibilities of mixing pattern with pattern are without limits. Here, a deep, square-backed sofa has been cleverly upholstered in different fabrics: the central panels display an antique Indian tree of life crewelwork with more pieces of the same crewelwork used to make up at set of matching pillows; the skirt around the base of the sofa is also picked out in the same fabric to give a fun ethnic look.**

This page **Other ethnic and textured patterns provide plenty of interest and can be used to inject color and life onto plain seating or used in with a medly of patterns to create a visual feast.**

springs to mind immediately, observe your everyday surroundings a bit more closely and you will be pleasantly surprised at how many mundane objects can be turned into stylish motifs. Another clever idea is to extrapolate a motif from an upholstery fabric and turn it into a stencil you can use to decorate the walls, the floor or even the ceiling—whatever surface takes your fancy.

If stenciling does not appeal, you could pick up a needle and try the decorative art of appliqué. To appliqué is literally to apply a second layer of fabric onto a base cloth by using either decorative stitching or glue to fix the appliqué into place, creating a pattern. Like many other forms of needlecraft, appliqué has

survived for generations and lends itself to all manner of designs. All you need to do is choose a motif, or series of motifs, draw and cut them out from scraps of fabrics and apply them to a background.

Motifs are all around us, and their use is limited only by our imagination. Make them work for you, in an almost infinite variety of ways, to create your own truly individual interior.

Both pages **Tribal kente cloth—this is a silk fabric made in Ghana by sewing together long narrow hand-woven strips. The beautifully bold kente design with its irregular geometrics works well on large surfaces and here is used on pillows and as a tablecloth, juxtaposed against elegant French furniture making a very chic contrast.**

Throughout the history of
human civilization, people
have always loved to
surround themselves with
pictorial symbols of
life, whether fairy-tale
figures, flora, or fauna, these
suggestive images animate
the process of decoration.

pictorial

SINCE THE TIME OF THE FIRST CAVE-DWELLERS, HUMAN BEINGS HAVE ENHANCED THEIR HOMES WITH PICTORIAL REPRESENTATIONS OF THE WORLD AROUND THEM.

In medieval times, the aristocracy delighted in tapestries which often depicted scenes from mythology or great feats of heroic achievement. Little has changed, and many of us still like to enhance our homes with charming pictorial designs.

It can be difficult to make a distinction between motifs and pictorial patterns as they have many elements in common, but it is probably useful to think of pictorial designs as being made up of many different component motif elements that join together to form an all-over pattern rhythm.

Due to their complexity, using pictorial patterns can seem intimidating. The trick is to spend some time thinking about how to use their high-impact nature to best advantage in your

Left **A pile of elegant classical pillows, from top to bottom: a simple printed *toile de Jouy* cover, an elegant stripe, and a small woven brocade.**
Above **A more unusual *toile de Jouy* with a red background is used on a lampshade which has been trimmed with braid, top and bottom.**

home. The best way to do this is to buy a yard or two of the fabric and match it up with the schemes in your home. See how the light affects the pattern, whether the sheer scale of the design is something you want to live with in quantity, or whether you might feel more comfortable using it to pick out one or two decorative features. Do not be tempted to take home a small swatch of the fabric as the beauty of these patterns is in the large-scale nature of its repeats, and you will not be able to get an accurate idea of the full impact from a scrap of fabric a few inches long. Admittedly, pictorial patterns are not as easy to use as some simpler patterns, but they can look ravishing and are much more versatile than they might at first appear. They can be used alone, mixed together with different patterns and textures, or used in conjunction with just one other pattern, such as a coordinating check or stripe.

Right and far right **In a sunny French bedroom, the walls are upholstered in a plain narrow stripe. The headboard and the bedcover are in a traditional pink** *toile de Jouy,* **and the plump pillows and simple curtains are picked out in a complementary small check. This demonstrates how highly pictorial toiles blend perfectly happily with geometrics as long as the color schemes also work.**

Near right **A period chair looks good with the seat upholstered in** *toile de Jouy* **fabric.**

The key to using pictorial designs in combination with other patterns is to find a color shared by both and to use this as a linking thread, unifying an otherwise random selection.

The desire for us to surround ourselves with pictorial patterns can be seen as a form of escapism from the drab, humdrum realities of daily life. We all have dreams and fantasies, and it is very tempting to surround ourselves with visual representations of our desires. A key example would be the extraordinary vogue for chinoiserie, which is a French term applied to Western interpretations of Chinese motifs. Until very recently, few Westerners ever traveled to China. The country, and its inhabitants, became the very embodiment of all things exotic. It comes as no surprise to find that chinoiserie patterns, in one form or another, have cropped up time and time again in the decorating schemes of the West. Chinoiserie was first popularized by the French court painter of the 18th century, Jean Baptiste Pillement, and by Madame de Pompadour, the mistress of Louis XV. The vogue for chinoiserie swept Europe, and every conceivable surface was covered in features which have since become shorthand for the exotic East—weeping willows, pagodas, arched bridges and paper lanterns. Furniture of all descriptions, porcelain, silver, garden buildings, plasterwork, silks, and tapestries; all were emblazoned with chinoiserie.

Far right **Large-scale pictorial patterns like** *toile de Jouy* **are often used as wall coverings in France. In fact, the French are crazy about** *toiles*. **As the cloth is made of fairly lightweight cotton, it needs to be interlined and can be suspended from wooden strips, attached to the walls. Here in a French hotel, the room has a unified look, with curtains and walls in matching colors of** *toile de jouy*.
Right **The chair is upholstered in various antique pink** *toiles*.

Having lapsed somewhat in popularity, the romanticized symbols of chinoiserie have, once again, become popular elements in contemporary interiors the world over.

Pictorial designs do not necessarily have to be as fantastic as full-scale chinoiserie. The floral chintzes and foliate designs long favored by the British are an ingenious way of conjuring up the illusion of having brought nature indoors. The shapes created by intertwining flowers and leaves offer a rich vein of decorative possibilities, from clearly demarcated formal patterns to rampantly wild naturalistic designs, and can be adapted to any style of interior. The Victorians adored decorating with florals, taking them to their hearts in myriad forms and a rainbow of bright colors. According to the jury of the Great Exhibition held in London in 1851 "The task is to cover the surface almost entirely with large, coarse flowers; dahlias, hollyhocks, roses, hydrangeas or others, which are often magnified by the designer much beyond the scale of nature".

applying fabric to walls

Lining walls with fabric is a lovely way to add pattern to a room, and it is no more difficult than decorating with wallpaper. It is particularly effective above a dado rail with a plain wall below, which highlights the pattern without taking over the entire room. Using a *toile de Jouy* creates a pastoral bower and is perfect for a small living room or a bedroom. Matching curtains and upholstery add to the sense of sophisticated comfort.

Materials and equipment

fabric for walls (see step 1 for amount)

thick interlining (see step 1 for amount)

braid to cover staples

plywood strip 1 x ½ inch (see step 1 for length)

fabric glue

scissors

upholstery staples

Measuring up

1 Measure the distance between the ceiling and dado rail to calculate the amount of fabric needed for each length to be attached to the wall. Add 2 inches to this for the hems at the top and bottom and add the length of the pattern repeat where necessary.

Next measure around the room, adding 2 inches for each corner and 1 inch each side of a door or window frame. Remember to include the space above each window and door. Divide this measurement by the width of your fabric (excluding the selvages) which will give you the number of lengths you require. Add the lengths together to calculate the total amount of fabric.

Calculate the amount of interlining you need in the same way, but do not add extra for the pattern repeat.

To calculate the amount of plywood strip needed to mount the fabric, measure all the way around the room, including windows and doors, and multiply by two.

Mounting the plywood strip

2 Cut the strip to length and screw to the top of the walls, above door and window frames and against the dado rail, as below.

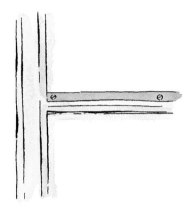

Attaching the interlining

3 Cut lengths of interlining, turn in 1 inch at the top and bottom, and staple them to the plywood strips. Tuck in well at the corners.

Attaching the fabric

4 For complex patterned fabrics, such as *toile de Jouy*, you need to cut each length of fabric as you apply it to the walls, as some sections need to be longer than others to make the pattern match up from panel to panel. Cut the first length so that a complete scene will fall at the level of the dado rail. Then working from a corner, turn under 1 inch at the top of the fabric and along the left hand selvage and staple this folded edge across the top strip. Keeping the fabric equally taut across the width, all the way down the length, turn under the excess fabric at the bottom and staple it to the lower strip, making sure it lies flat against the wall, with no puckers or wrinkles.

5 Cut the next length, carefully matching the pattern. Turn under the top inch and the left hand selvage, and carefully matching the pattern, place this edge over the selvage of the first length. Staple at the top and bottom.

6 Repeat this process until you reach a corner. The length should then be cut to the right width to reach the corner plus a 1-inch seam allowance. Attach this length in the usual way, but turn in both long sides; keep the right-hand side well tucked into the corner. Use the fabric that you cut off the previous length for the next length and abut it right up to the previous length.

7 Continue working around the room with your *toile de Jouy*, cutting the fabric carefully to fit around window frames and doors; always allow an extra inch of fabric to turn under against both the sides of the frames and to attach to the plywood strip at the top of the frames.

Attaching the braid

8 Glue the braid along the top of the wall and above the dado rail to cover the staples.

Fabric walls can also be attached with special dado rails, that fit over the edges of the fabric, as right.

Botanical prints are another example of those design classics which never seem to lose their appeal. Currently enjoying a revival engendered by a growing interest in the environment and all things green, these designs work surprisingly well in almost every room. Botanicals work well as wall coverings, curtains, and slipcovers. If you can lay your hands on some inexpensive reproductions of botanical prints, they look marvelous pasted onto a screen or hung in a decorative arrangement as if they were a group of genuine prints. This idea works beautifully with any type of decorative print, as long as you stick to a theme. They could be Indian miniatures, shells, or prints of birds, whatever appeals to you. Don't feel you have to frame these pictures—throw convention to the wind, as they are pretty enough in their own right to defy the need for gilded frames. You might even want to consider covering an entire room in antique prints (see the examples on pages 182–3).

Perhaps unsurprisingly, many of our contemporary pictorial patterns have their origins on the India subcontinent. The East India Company first began to import painted and dyed Indian cloths during the 17th century, and they soon became *de rigueur* in fashionable circles. Greatly admired for their bright, fast colors and intricate designs, they were much in demand for both furnishings and clothing. Needless to say, imitators

Above left **Above an 18th-century bed hangs a large corona with *toile de Jouy* cascading down and spilling over the bed.**
Right **A bedroom is given the classical *toile de Jouy* treatment; the canopied half-tester, bedspread, and walls are all in the same reproduction of an 18th-century *toile*. Plain white antique bed linen, black and white floor tiles, an oval relief picture, and the soft bobble fringe serve to break up the vast sea of pattern.**

Left and below **A navy-blue reproduction** *toile* **is glued onto the walls and ceiling to liven up an architecturally featureless bedroom. The broad French stripe on the window shades and draperies contrasts well.**

Right **A lighter treatment for** *toile de Jouy.* **The modern four-poster is dressed with lime-green** *toile* **that has been used sparingly.**

quickly sprang up all over Europe, notably in Holland, France, and England. Daniel Defoe writing in 1708 observes that decorated cottons "…had crept into our houses; our closets and bed-chambers, curtains, cushions, chairs and at last beds themselves, were nothing but callicoes and Indian stuffs."

The tree of life is a pattern whose design has been strongly influenced by mythology. First brought to the West from India in the 17th century, it has been employed in sophisticated settings ever since, lining passageways in French farmhouses and used to make slipcovers for the library

chairs in one of England's famous homes, Longleat House in Wiltshire. Early in the 19th century, at the height of the pattern's popularity, the English porcelain factory, Coalport, produced a line known as Indian tree which was based on the tree of life design. Although the tree of life takes many forms, the common features are a central stem or tree trunk with stylized foliage, although these are not necessarily rendered in their natural colors. This style of pattern is usually found printed onto cotton or glazed chintz and the tree of life motif itself has evolved over the years to include other motifs, making it a much richer pattern. Depending on the personal preferences of the designer, contemporary trees might feature birds of paradise, pomegranates, butterflies, and exotic fruit, all set against a lush background of flowing tendrils and sinuous stems.

Left **A Parisian living room-cum-study is decorated in a warm, rich red *toile de Jouy*. The high-impact *toile* mixes effortlessly with red striped curtains and inviting wool pillows. Because there are so many variations of *toiles de Jouy*, now available in an infinity of color choices, it is an extremely adaptable pattern. You can engulf an entire room in it or just use it to cover a single pillow. It is such a pretty material you can never have too much of it.**

Above **Old *toiles* with floral designs were traditionally printed with woodblocks and known as "indiennes".** The pattern is full of movement and life without over-powering the room. An overscaled tree of life *toile indienne* in a single color is used for an all-over look. Right **A rich chocolate medallion *toile de Jouy* looks good used against soft fruitwood furniture and plain white painted paneled doors and windows.**

As with many of the pictorial patterns, the tree of life tends to have a large-scale repeat, making it hard to visualize what the final result will look like. Don't let this fact deter you. This is such a pretty and attractive pattern that its scale never seems to matter, and it tends not to dominate in the way that a bold stripe might. It works very well used alone, but it also looks good mixed with a medley of different types of fabrics and patterns. It is even feasible to use a damask, a small stripe, a plain weave, and a tree of life all in the same room, as long as you unify the composition by choosing a dominant color. Once you have chosen your color, you can have fun mixing and matching fabrics,

Right **This is an example of decorating with *toile* at its most powerful. The fabric is beautifully printed with strong colors and clear, dynamic outlines. It needs very little else added—a six-paned French door to a terrace stands alongside a simple stripe in complementary colors on a chair.** Far right **The open door reveals lozenge shapes carved into its surface, that stand out against the *toile* wallpaper.**

wallpapers, flooring, and furniture. The tree of life looks great for slipcovers on a group of chairs, because due to the large scale, it is possible to alter the repeat of the pattern slightly on the various chairs, providing the eye with a pleasant variety of forms.

Since time immemorial people have been puzzling over how to incorporate pattern in fabrics by means other than weaving or dyeing. It comes as no surprise that it was in India that someone first had the ingenuity to devise a means of decorating fabric using engraved wooden blocks similar to those used for printing woodcut book illustrations. By the late Middle Ages, block printing had become an established trade in Europe, particularly in Italy and Germany. More sophisticated methods of printing onto cloth, however, took a while to evolve. It was not until 1752 that a certain Francis Nixon of Drumcondra in Ireland was smart enough to realize it was possible to use copper plates as a means of applying pattern to textiles. He described his results as having "All the advantages of light and shade, in the strongest and most lasting colors." By the time of the early 1760s, there were several factories around London producing high-quality copperplate prints. The English and Irish nearly had a complete monopoly on all the copperplate printing up until the arrival of Christophe-Philippe Oberkampf. A German national, Oberkampf was working in Switzerland when he was invited to Paris to help with the establishment of a new print works. In 1760, he opened his own factory at Jouy-en-Jousas, a small village on the outskirts of Paris, and had to import a team of overseas experts to train his staff. Clearly a man of great ingenuity, he traveled widely, inspecting other printing factories and adapting their innovations for use in his own. Oberkampaf actually introduced copperplate printing techniques to his factory in 1770. Best known for printing *toile de*

Jouy, surely one of the most wonderful fabrics ever invented, by 1797 Oberkampf was printing 5,000 yards of printed cloth a day, which in that era was considered a staggering achievement. In 1806, Oberkampf was awarded the *Legion d'honneur* by Napoleon I.

Although once specific to the fabrics produced by Oberkampf's factory, the term *toile de Jouy* has come to be universally applied to monochrome figurative designs, wherever they might come from and as they have become increasingly popular the world over the designs and colors have multiplied. A traditional *toile* is usually printed on cotton, or sometimes linen, in one color on a natural or off-white background. The colors used for *toiles* are usually red, sepia, deep purple, or a rich indigo-blue. The most traditional *toiles* featured arcadian scenes of pastoral simplicity, but as the genre grew in popularity, a demand arose for the depiction of episodes from popular literary works, such as Robinson Crusoe and Don Quixote, and representations of topical events—the American War of Independence and the Montgolfier brothers' first balloon ascent of 1783 were particularly popular.

In addition to printing the fabrics we now know as *toile de Jouy*, Oberkampf's factory was also turning out floral designs, printed by the traditional woodblock methods, which were known as indiennes. These

Top left **A whimsical leaf and stem design which benefits from some natural greenery.**
Above and right **Delicate chinoiserie subtly painted pale lemon yellow creates a calm and sophisticated background for modern sculpture and classical furniture.**
Far right **Giant climbing floral motifs with a Chinese flavor are elaborately painted in strong colors on a Paris dining-room wall with plates hung around the pattern.**

Below **Below dado level, panels are painted with urns of flowers in Gripsholm Castle in Sweden.** Right **Dramatic patterns are repeated on the walls and curtains.** Far right **Panels of *toile* are used to decorate a bedroom.**

latter fabrics accounted for the largest part of the factory's output, reaching a crescendo of popularity under the patronage of Napoleon's empress, Josephine. Heavily influenced by the traditional Indian and Persian textiles, indiennes often incorporated birds and other rococo motifs such as fluttering ribbons or garlands. Before Josephine's enthusiasm for Oberkampf's indiennes, Marie-Antoinette had actually decorated her pastoral retreat at

Versailles, Le Hameau, in swathes of *toile de Jouy*. Napoleon liked it so much that he lined his campaign tents with the fabric. In fact, it is fair to say that, ever since the textile's inception, the French have always been crazy about *toile*. It is only fairly recently, however, that the rest of the world has latched onto the sheer prettiness and versatility of *toile de Jouy* as a decorating fabric. The great thing about it is that you can use as little or as much as you like.

All cultures share a strong tradition of delight in the narrative. Surrounding yourself with pictorial pattern is a delicious, and surprisingly easy, way of immersing yourself in fantasy. You can use a different style of pattern for each room in your house so that every space has a different story to tell.

Far left **The wonderful intricacy, vivid colors, and perfect detail of many botanical and mogul prints provide us with all kinds of decorative possibilities. In this guest twin bedroom even rows of botanical prints have been used with wit and precision to lend pictorial decoration to the walls. This is a novel variation on the theme of the period print room. The prints are glued to the wall and then laminated to give the impression of being painted and to provide an all-over smooth surface. The coverlets on the beds echo the botanical theme.**

Above left **The same technique of gluing and lamination has been used on Indian prints.**

Right **Glorious 17th-century drawings by the Swedishman Karl von Linné, who was a leading botanist of his time, have been crudely pasted onto wood planked walls in his study outside Uppsala.**

Suppliers
Credits and Glossary
Index
Acknowledgments

resources

Items marked with an asterisk (*) are available only through architects and interior designers.

Fabrics, trims, and wallpaper

B & J Fabric
263 West 40th Street
New York, NY 10018
Natural fiber fabrics. Call or write for samples. Search and special-order services.

Beacon Hill
979 Third Avenue
New York, NY 10022
Broad selection of printed and woven fabrics available.

Bennison Fabrics
76 Green Street
New York, NY 10012
Wide variety of decorating fabrics.

Boussac of France *
979 Third Avenue
New York, NY 10022
Cotton printed and woven fabrics in a variety of natural fibers.

Brunschwig & Fils *
979 Third Avenue
New York, NY 10022
Wide variety of printed and woven fabrics in a variety of natural fibers.

Calico Corners
203 Gale Lane
Kennett Square
PA, 19348
Fabrics, mail order, and catalog.

Manuel Canovas *
136 East 57th Street
New York, NY 10022
Selection of stylish floral prints and a wide range of woven, colorful fabrics.

Clarence House Fabrics, Ltd. *
211 East 58th Street
New York, NY 10022
Printed natural fiber fabrics based on documents from the 15th-20th centuries. Hand-woven textiles and opulent trims.

Conso Products
P.O. Box 326
Union, SC 29379
Enormous collection of trims, tassels, and fringes of all types.

Covington Fabrics *
15 East 26th Street
New York
NY 10010
Extensive range of classic and fashion-forward fabrics in a variety of fibers.

Cowtan & Tout, Inc *
(distributors for Jane churchill and Colefax & Fowler)
979 Third Avenue
New York, NY 10022
Traditional fabrics and wallcoverings from silk brocades to prints on linens as well as bright contemporary ones.

Donghia *
379 Third Avenue
New York, NY 10022
Broad selection of fabrics and trimmings.

The Fabric Center
485 Electric Avenue
Fitchburg
MA 01420
A wide variety of decorator fabrics mail order and catalog available.

Garnet Hill
P.O. Box 262
Main Street, Franconia
NH 03580
Natural fibers and bed linen.

Hinson & Co *
979 Third Avenue
New York, NY 10022
Fabrics and coordinating wallcoverings with emphasis on clean designs.

Houles Inc *
8584 Melrose Avenue
Los Angeles, CA 90069
Luxurious handmade imported trimmings of all sorts.

Keepsake Quilting
Route 25B
P.O. Box 1618
Center Harbor
NH 03226-1618
Good selection of lightweight cottons, threads, and notions. Mail order and catalog available.

Ian Mankin
at Agnes Bourne, Showroom 220
2 Henry Adams Street
San Francisco, CA
941031022
Good value cotton fabrics in a variety of colors and patterns.

Marvic Textiles *
979 Third Avenue
New York, NY 10022
Wide range of upholstery textures in bright colors.

Mombasa Net Canopies
2345 Fort Worth Street
Grand Prairie
Texas, 75050
Mosquito nets for bedhangings.

Oppenheim's
P.O. Box 29
120 East Main Street
North Manchester
IN 46962-0052
Country prints, mill remnants, denim, chambray, flannels. Swatches on request, mail order and catalog available.

Osborne & Little
(distributors for Designer's Guild)
979 Third Avenue
New York, NY 10022
Broad selection of printed and woven fabrics and wallcoverings.

Pierre Deux
570 Madison Avenue
New York, NY 10021
French Provincial printed fabrics and custom drapery service. Mail order available.

Portico Bed & Bath
139 Spring Street
New York, NY 10012
Beautiful white linens and throws.

Ralph Lauren Home
979 Third Avenue
New York, NY 10022
980 Madison Avenue
New York, NY 10021
867 Madison Avenue
New York, NY 10021
Broad selection of printed and woven fabrics, wallcoverings and trimmings.

Rosebrand Textiles
517 West 35th Street
New York, NY
Gauze, canvas and ticking fabrics.

Sanderson *
979 Third Avenue
New York, NY 10022
Good quality upholstery fabrics.

F. Schumacher & Co *
79 Madison Avenue
New York
NY 10016
Extensive selection of fabrics in various fibers and coordinating trims.

Scalamandre Silk, Inc. *
950 Third Avenue
New York, NY 10022
Leading restorer of classic document fabrics. Trims, wallpaper, custom carpets.

Smith & Noble
P.O. Box 1387
Corona
CA 91718
Vertical and horizontal shades and blinds in all materials, Roman shades, cornice boxes. Mail order and catalog available.

Waverly Fabrics *
79 Madison Avenue
New York, NY 10016
Broad selection of printed and woven fabrics in natural fibers. Coordinating accessories and wallpaper borders.

Williamsburg Catalog
The Colonial Williamsburg
Foundation
Department 023
P.O. Box 3532
Williamsburg, VA 23187
Colonial style furniture and fabrics such as checked blankets.

Curtain Hardware

Country Curtains
The Red Lion Inn
Stockbridge
MA 01262
Extensive assortment of hardware and wide selection of fabric, swags and accessories. Mail order and catalog available.

Kirsch
P.O. Box 0370
Sturgis
MI 49091
Enormous selection of curtain and drapery hardware, rods, fabric window coverings, and blinds.

Spring Window Fashions
7549 Graber Road
Middleton, WI 53562
Vinyl, metal, and fabric vertical and horizontal blinds and shades. Mail order and catalog available.

The Warm Company
954 East Union
Seattle
WA 98122
Specialising in insulated fabric for window shades and curtains, contact the above address for your nearest outlet.

Paint Supplies

Benjamin Moore & Co.
51 Chestnut Ridge Road
Montvale
NJ 07645
Selection of paints and stains for the home, including good period-style colors in muted shades.

Charrette Favor Ruhl
31 Olympia Avenue
Woburn
MA 01888
Painting materials and paints for interiors and exteriors.

Janovic
30-35 Thompson Avenue
Long Island City
NY 11101
Good selection of paints in a broad color range to suit most interiors.

Home Depot
449 Roberts Court Road
Kennisaw
GA 30144
Paint color, equipment and materials.

Pearl Paint Co.
306 Canal Street
New York, NY 10013
Many different paint colors to choose from for home decorating.

Pittsburgh Paints
PPG Industies Inc.
1 PPG Place
Pittsburgh, PA 15272
Good color range of paints.

Pratt & Lambert
75 Townawanda Street
Buffalo
New York, NY 142007
Lots of colors, plus a good selection of off-whites.

Ralph Lauren Paint
980 Madison Avenue
New York, NY 10021
Vast range of colorful paints, separated into sections that follow a particular theme such as River Rock, Desert, and the Hollywood Collection.

Sherwin Williams
101 Prospect Avenue
Cleveland, OH
44115
Good selection of colors for any style of interior.

Flooring Specialists

Albro Sisal
8807 Beverly Blvd.
Los Angeles
CA 90048

Bruce Hardwood Floors
16803 Dallas Parkway
Dallas
Texas
75248

The Carpet and Rug Institute
P.O. Box 2048
Dalton
GA 30722

Country Floors
8735 Melrose Avenue
Los Angeles, CA 90069

Decorative Wood Floors
8687 Melrose Avenue
West Hollywood
CA 90069

Johnsonite
A division of Duramex Inc.
16910 Munn Road
Chagrin Fall
CA 90048

Hoechst Celanese
1211 Avenue of the Americas
New York, NY 10036

Plaza Hardwood Inc.
5 Enebra Court
Santa Fe, NM 87505

The Rug Barn
P.O. Box 1187
Abbeville, SC 29620

S & S Mills
2650 Lakeland Road SE
Dalton
GA 30721

Barbara Zinkel
333 Pilgrim
Birmingham, MI 48009

credits

Interior Designers
whose work appears in the book:

Carla Bavoretti (architect)
2 Via Vico
10128 Torino
Italy
See pages: 46, 59, 124, 125

Ngila Boyd
See pages: 22 bottom left, 25 middle
right, 33, 96, 97 bottom right

Reed Boyd
Contact Jonathan Reed
151a Sydney Street
London
SW3
See pages: 22 bottom right, 23, 57

Mary Drysdale
1733 Connecticut Avenue NW
Washington DC 20009
USA
See pages: 4, 5, 13, 14, 15, 18, 19,
48–50, 58 top and bottom right, 63,
76, 98, 99, 102, 103, 106, 107, 109,
120, 121, 126–7, 128 right, 129,
131, 148, 149, 171, 178 top and
bottom right

Laura Geas
Ciel Decor, 187 New Kings Road
London SW6
See pages: 146, 147

Patrice Gruffaz
Shop: Lieux
21 boulevard Henri IV
Paris 75004
See pages: 8, 9, 51 left, 56, 156–7,
172–3

Allegra and Ashley Hicks
33 Bywater Street
London
SW3
See pages: 24, 25 top left and right
and bottom right, 32, 46, 59, 97 left
and top right, 118, 123–5, 128 left,
133, 152–5, 182

John McCall
Meadow House
Chapel Road
Bucklebury
Berkshire
See pages: 51 top and bottom right

Christopher Moore
1 Munro Terrace
Cheyne Walk
London
SW10
See pages: 168 right top and bottom,
169

Mimmi O'Connell
Shop: Port of Call
Walton Street
London SW7
See pages: 20, 21, 28, 36, 38 left and
bottom right, 95, 150 center, 151,
170

Anne Porée
Bernard Bourret
Shop: 5 Rue du Limas
Avignon 84000
France
See page: 168 top left

Richard Ronald
c/o Manuel Canovas
2 North Terrace
London
SW3
See pages: 119, 132, 150 left and
right, 174 left and bottom

Steven Ryan
Design and Decoration
60 Ledbury Road
London
W11
See pages: 17 right, 30, 31, 94

Gerald schmorl
Fax for enquiries: Paris 1 4878 4120
See pages: 22 top and center, 37,
41–3, 52–55, 179

Melissa Wyndham
6 Sydney Street
London
SW3
See pages: 112, 113

Other locations
where photographs were taken:

Bill Blass
New York
US
See pages: 16, 17 top and left, 44, 45,
47

Chateau de Barbentane
near Avignon, France
Open to the public
See pages: 138 right and bottom, 139,
180 right

Glamis Castle
Forfar
Scotland
Open to the public
See pages: 112, 113

Gripsholm Castle
Mariefred
Sweden
Open to the public
See pages: 29, 58 top and bottom left,
68 left and right, 86, 104, 105, 136,
137, 138 left and center, 180 left

Hotel de la Mirande
Avignon, France
See pages: 12, 26, 27, 64, 65 left, 66
right, 71, 78, 144–5, 160 middle,
161, 164, 165, 167, 174 right,
175–7, 178 top left

Hotel Villa Gallici
Aix en Provence, France
See pages: 65 middle and right, 66
right, 67 left, 70, 73, 74, 75, 77, 89,
110, 111, 162, 163, 181

Linnaeus Hammarby Museum
Uppsala
Sweden
Open to the public
See pages: 61 top left and bottom
right, 134, 135, 183

Johan & Madelein Norden
Sweden
See pages: 38 top right, 39, 66 top
and bottom left, 92 bottom left, 114

Sudeley Castle Furniture
The Dairy Farm
Sudeley Castle
Cheltenham
Gloucestershire
Bed available from Sudeley Castle
Furniture
See page: 51 top right

Svindersvik
Nacka
Stockholm
Open to the public
See pages: 60, 61 bottom left, 84, 85,
87, 88, 92 top left and right, 93

Lillian Williams
Chateau in Normandy
France
See pages: 68 middle, 69, 140, 141,
143

glossary

Appliqué stitching a second layer of fabric onto a base cloth.

Art Nouveau a decorative style, developed in the 1880s, and characterized by floral and leaf motifs.

Bargello a type of needlepoint or tapestry stitch with a zigzag pattern.

Bias the diagonal line on a piece of fabric running from selvage to selvage for maximum stretch.

Bolster a cylindrical cushion.

Brocade a rich, woven fabric with a matte background. Traditionally made from silk or cotton.

Buttoning a buttoned quilted effect found on padded upholstery.

Campaign style features of the temporary military shelter and transportable furniture used by armies.

Canopy a covering hung over a bed.

Chaise longue a couch with a back and a short armrest at one end.

Chinoiserie decoration, ornaments, and furniture made in Europe in the Chinese style.

Chintz a cotton fabric, sometimes polished, printed in several colors on a pale or white background.

Coir natural coconut fiber.

Colonial style architecture, furniture design, and decoration from 17th-century North American.

Cornice a plaster molding covering the join between the wall top and the ceiling.

Corona a structure fitted to the wall above a headboard, to hang draperies.

Crewelwork hard-wearing fabric woven with a closely twisted yarn made from combed wool and embroidered in chain or herringbone stitch.

Dado rail this rail runs around the walls of a room just above waist height.

Damask woven figured material, originally silk but often linen, cotton, or wool.

Fauteuil French for an armchair.

Faux a French word meaning false.

Figurative design representing a figure, emblem, or symbol.

Fleur de lys a heraldic floral motif that originated in France.

Fortuny a richly textured Italian cloth with patterning made with wax-resistant techniques.

Gaufrage velvet a velvet with an embossed texture created by engraved, heated rollers.

Gauze a fine, soft cotton fabric in a plain, loose weave.

Gilding a technique for applying gold directly to surfaces.

Gingham traditional checked fabric woven in white with one other color.

Gothic originating from the 11th and 15th centuries, this style features slender lines and pointed arches.

Herringbone a twill weave made by alternating a diagonal pattern in the cloth.

Homespun unsophisticated fabric, traditionally spun at home rather than machine-made.

Ikat fabric that is patterned by resist-dyeing.

Linen a robust cloth made from flax.

Miter where two ends of a strip are folded and hemmed into a diagonal seam.

Madder a plant whose root gives a natural red dye.

Madras a thin cotton fabric in brightly colored checks or stripes.

Matelasse a thick, double cloth, woven with double sets of warp and weft threads and interlined.

Moiré silk taffeta cloth with a water-marked effect made by engraved rollers.

Neoclassical style a style of decoration and architecture based on the forms of ancient Greece and Rome.

Organdy hard-wearing finely woven thin cotton or gauze.

Organza transparently thin fabric made of silk, rayon, or nylon.

Paisley derived from shawls imported from India and then produced in Paisley in Scotland, features highly-stylized floral motifs.

Piping cord that is covered with bias binding strips to decorate edges.

Piqué stiff, ribbed woven cotton, similar to twill, usually in white.

Plaid a long piece of wool cloth usually in tartan.

Print any cloth which has a colored design added by a mechanical process.

Provençal print brightly colored French country prints covered with small motifs and floral designs.

Regency style a style found in England between 1790 and 1837.

Sari a Hindu woman's dress; long cloth is wrapped around the waist and passed over the shoulder and head.

Satin closely woven silk with a shiny surface, matte on the reverse.

Scallop a border or heading cut into deep round, semicircles.

Sheer any thin and translucent fabric which filters light.

Silk taffeta plain, woven cloth with subtle ribs across the width.

Sisal a coarse natural fiber suitable for flooring and matting.

Stenciling a decorative technique where paint is applied to a surface through a cutout design.

Swag a decorative arrangement of fabric at the top of a window.

Swatch a small sample of fabric, wall color, or wallpaper.

Tapestry an ornamental textile used for covering walls and furniture.

Tartan a distinctive checked plaid pattern in wool or other cloth pertaining to a Highland clan.

Ticking heavy cotton twill fabric, often with a herringbone texture, originally used for covering pillows and mattresses.

Tieback a form of loop, anchored to the wall which pulls a curtain away to the edge of the window.

Toile de Jouy the name derives from an 18th-century factory in Jouy-en-Josas, France. They are cotton prints in a single color on a natural or off-white background.

Trefoil a three-lobed form similar to a clover leaf.

Trim a decorative finish to any type of furnishing accessory.

Tweed a rough woolen cloth used for making suits and jackets, originating from Tweed, in northern England.

Twill a woven fabric showing distinct diagonal lines.

Valance a decorative device hung above curtains to hide the track.

Vellum fine parchment prepared in lime baths and derived from calf's skin.

Velvet silk fabric with a soft, short pile and a luxurious texture.

Vitruvian scroll a Greek form of ornamentation, like the profile of a wave on the point of breaking.

Waffle weave a surface texture like the gridlike pattern on a waffle cake.

Warp the lengthwise threads on a loom, interlaced by the weft threads to create woven cloth.

Weave the texture of a woven fabric, created by interlacing threads.

Weft the crosswise threads on a loom interlaced by the warp threads to create woven cloth.

index

acknowledgments

Many thanks to **James Merrell** for his exceptionally high standard of photographs. A big thanks to **Amicia de Moubray** who wrote the main text for the book with inexhaustable energy and professionalism.

Thanks to all the people who kindly opened their houses to us; among them **Madelein** and **Johan Norden, Ashley** and **Allegra Hicks, Mary Drysdale, Gerald schmorl, Ngila Boyd, Christopher Moore, Mimmi O'Connell, Bill Blass, Lillian Williams, Patrice Gruffaz, Stephen Ryan, Laura Geas,** and **Richard Ronald**. Many thanks to **Monsieur** and **Madame Stein**, owners of La Mirande Hotel in Avignon and to **Monsieur Jouve** at the Hotel Gallici in Aix en Provence, and to all the **museum curators**, most especially at Svindersvik in Stockholm and Gripsholm Castle in Mariefried, Sweden.

To my friends who are always on hand for help, advice and childcare; **Janey Joicey-Cecil, Dasha Shenkman, Carol Glasser, Mary Emmerling, Anna Thomas,** and **Jane Cumberbatch**.

To **Catherine Coombes**, as always, who holds this little office of mine together with enthusiasm and fun.

Finally to **David** and **Harry** and the rest of my family, all of whom mean everything to me.

credits for the projects

The projects in the book were inspired by the following people; **Mary Drysdale** for the painted kitchen wall, Greek key border and the stenciled floor border. **Gerald schmorl** for the painted striped ceiling, **Ashley Hicks** for the Roman blind with decorative swirls, **Lillian Williams** for the garlanded painted panel, **Hotel Villa Gallici** in Aix en Provence for the decorative bordered curtains, and **Hotel de la Mirande** in Avignon for the *toile* on walls project.